T0065528

Four-Leaf Clover

Four-Leaf Clover

A Down Syndrome Portrait

John Schissler, Jr.

Rev. date: 02/12/2021

To order additional copies of this book, contact:
Xlibris
844-714-8691
www.Xlibris.com
Orders@Xlibris.com
822794

CONTENTS

Introduction xi

Stage 1: Disbelief..1

Stage 2: Grief 7

Stage 3: Hope..13

Stage 4: Awareness..23

Stage 5: Respite 29

LIFE WITH ADAM

Vignette 1: Love-Ins 39

Vignette 2: Poster Child...43

Vignette 3: "Peach Inspediment" 47

Vignette 4: Journey..51

Vignette 5: Holy Emanations!................................59

Vignette 6: Tv or Not Tv?..63

Vignette 7: In Sickness and in Health.........................69

Vignette 8: Oops! 75

Vignette 9: Exceptional Group 81

Vignette 10: Exceptional Tours................................87

Vignette 11: Girls, Girls, Girls 93

Vignette 12: All in the Family 99

Vignette 13: Oldies But Goodies 105

Vignette 14: Red-Letter Days 111

Vignette 15: Avant Savant 117

Vignette 16: Dealing with Loss 123

Vignette 17: The Apple of Our Eye 131

Epilogue 139

Addendum 147

Source Notes 149

PHOTOS

1. Daughter Angela, son Jeff, and my beautiful wife Barbara, 7 months pregnant xviii

2. Brother Jeff and sister Angela (not the nun) with papoose Adam 3

3. A quiet moment with my newborn Adam in the summer of '78 5

4. Adam getting a much-needed hug from Mom and Curious George...11

5. Adam (on the left) with cousin Philip on their 1st birthdays.... 19

6. Adam, seated with Easter Seal Ambassador Pat Thomas, with Emmett Prosser who was the 1981 co-poster child for Easter Seal. 25

7. Enjoying his life as a happy three-year-old..........................27

8. In the stands at the Special Olympics State Meet.................32

9. New home with our daughter's family. Adam's room is left of the front door..35

11. Some of Adam's photo ops as poster child for Easter Seals.....44

12. Adam sporting his "Where's the Beef? Pin 48

13. Checking out the Best Western pool in Salida, Colorado 53

14. Donald Duck scared Adam with his well-known "peach inspediment" 56

15. Some scary characters trying to escape the Haunted Mansion thumb-how 57

16. Brother Jeff donning his altar boy apparel at
     Christmas Eve Mass..59
17. On one of those sleepless nights with an ailing Adam
     with his pet bunny...71
18. Caught red-handed using Dad's camera while
     inventing the first "selfie".......................................76
19. Adam's early, insatiable need to plink around on a piano....82
20. The cover from one of the benefit booklets featuring
     the chorus 84
21. Adam wearing a satisfied smile after one of the
     Christmas concerts 85
22. The Chorus made the TV news for one of their
     recent benefit Xmas concerts.*...............................87
23. Adam singing "Achy-Breaky Heart" at one of his
     many performances...88
24. Adam as Tevia singing and dancing to "If I Were a
     Rich Man (1997)..89
25. The "Wholesome Kid" from Milwaukee, Wisconsin.........94
26. Adam's family: Mom, Dad, brother, sister, in-laws,
     niece and nephews. 99
27. Three generations of Schisslers in front of my
     ancestral home in Croatia 101
29. "It's not what's under the Christmas tree that
     matters, it's who's around it".* Charlie Brown..................111
30. "Mosaic" Adam ~Life is like a box of Crayons...................115
31. Adam toasting his brother and his sister-in-law Molly......120
32. Our 4-Leaf Clover with one of his outside toys on a
     beautiful fall day 131
33. Adam showing some love to his nephew Carlos
     when he was just a youngster.................................134
34. Adam with his very own extraordinary (ET) heartlight......137

Dedicated to my wife Barbara,
the most devoted spouse, friend, and mother.

INTRODUCTION

♪ "I'm looking over a four-leaf clover ♣
I've overlooked before
One leaf is sunshine, the second is rain
Third is the roses that grow in the lanes
No need explaining, the one remaining
Is someone we adore"...Adam *

*See Source Notes (footnote & bibliographies)

"Please be patient. God isn't finished with me yet" is the best advice I can give to any parent who is suddenly faced with the prospect of raising a child with Down syndrome. An engraved wooden sign with that reminder sat on the top of our newborn's dresser for his first six years in his room. As parents, Barbara and I learned that patience along with the correct information, was the best approach to address all of the fears we initially harbored when all we ever wished for was "a healthy baby". However, ignorance and misinformation often caused us to doubt. That doubt, then, frequently turned into fear. And, indeed, there was much misinformation out there in 1978, when our son was born. Unfortunately, some of that misinformation still follows us to this day. Fortunately, though, for parents in the 21st century, modern science has dispelled many of those misconceptions which used to stoke that fear.

Our son Adam was born on April 2, 1978, and he has been living with us in our home since then. Even with his birth, his arrival proved that Adam had a sense of humor. My pregnant wife Barbara had to make a trip to the hospital the day before. In spite of all the indications that he was ready to come into this world, he played an April Fools trick on her with a false alarm. A very disappointed Barb returned to our home on the north side of Milwaukee. Was it possible that he was waiting for me to come back from Italy the next day?

At the beginning of the 1977 school year, I was approached by the administration and asked if I would be interested in taking a number of my Latin students to Italy during the spring break in the following year. The opportunity was also given to my wife, who would be the chaperone for the female students who came along. As a Latin lover, I jumped at the opportunity to visit the Eternal City and the birthplace of the Romans' language. I signed an agreement for responsibilities that came with the eight days In Italy. Barb and I were so excited at the prospect of seeing Rome, Florence, and Venice...a life's dream come true.

But life reminds us to be ready for anything. About a month later, Barb found out that she was pregnant and the birth date was at the end of March of 1978. There was no way now that an almost nine month pregnant woman should go on a nine hour plane ride to Italy, much less walk about on some of the ancient streets in those old cities. But, because these were my students, I was not allowed to be released from my contract. So, the upcoming spring break was going to be bittersweet.

I felt like I had betrayed my wife those entire eight days and seven nights in Italy. The only consolation I could find was taking in the ancient Roman structures. They were far more massive and magnificent than photos could ever reveal. While I was losing sleep in Roma, Firenza, and Venezia, Barb was spending nervous nights at home due to my absence. The false labor pains didn't help calm her nerves either. I was particularly concerned that I was going to miss my *Bambino's* birth which was already a week late.

As soon as the plane's wheels were down, I went to my car and raced to the nearby hospital after hearing on the phone that Barb was there with labor pains. As soon as I rushed into the maternity ward at 2 a.m., I heard cheers erupting at the nurses station. Adam was born a half hour later.

Maybe getting only about 30 hours of sleep for those seven nights in Europe combined with the jet lag was responsible for what happened right after my arrival. I can still remember how surreal that hospital visit was. This wasn't my first rodeo, but the waiting room was more like a twilight zone. When the nurse brought our newborn to me, I was taken aback because it felt like I was looking at myself when I was a baby. Surreal, because my parents had no baby pictures of me because all was lost to them in postwar Europe. Everything just seemed so dream-like. All future looks at my son's face, inexplicably, didn't produce that same sensation again.

There was no April Fools trick played on us because Adam had waited for my arrival. But, fooled we weren't by the prospect of the special efforts required for raising a special needs child. The knowledge of those challenges would slowly and inexorably unfold for us in the following weeks, months, and year. And, if that wasn't challenging enough, we were going to have to face and put up with some of the most hurtful and disconcerting labels prescribed to Adam's condition, most notably, in the field of psychology. The most common label was "Mongolism", which psychologists categorized Mongoloids (Downs people) into three IQ levels:

"idiot" (0-25)
"imbecile"(26-50) and
"moron"(51-70),
(using 100 as the bell curve IQ of the average person)

Finally, "cretin", "feeble-minded", and "simpleton" were thrown in just for good measure. Many decades later "mentally retarded" became the label du jour followed by "intellectually disbabled" and, then, well you get the picture. My wiser and more intuitive wife Barbara had her own opinion about these labels from the very beginning: "Mongoloids are not idiots! Only the people who label them are!"

I hope the reader noticed that I called Adam's Down syndrome a "condition and not a "disease", which so many people used to say that he "suffered from". The term Down syndrome has its origins with John Langdon Down (1828-1896), a British physician who identified this genetic condition already in 1862. Doctor Langdon **Down** drew attention mostly to the physical features of the eyes shared by those cognitively disabled children like Adam. The term used was "slanted eyes". Because of this commonality, the term "Mongolism" was continued to be used by the medical profession for the following dozen decades.

However, according to the "Journal of Contemporary Anthropology, "Too much has been made of the folds at the corners of the eyes and of the supposed 'slanting eyes' associated with the term 'Mongoloid child'. Even among Chinese children, the characteristics of Down syndrome are not marked by the racial features.(Tsuang & Lin, 1964). Because the resemblance to Mongoloid people is slight and because the term carries negative connotations to many people, the older term has generally been discarded in favor of Down syndrome." *

Actually there are over 50 clinical characteristics which persons with Down syndrome may have. Some are less noticeable or less common in Downs. However, in 1973 in order to cause less confusion, editor Lloyd M. Dunn in the book *Exceptional Children in the Schools,* created a list of the 13 most common physical signs of Down syndrome:

1. Large fissured tongue
2. Short squared hands

3. Epicanthal fold at the inner core of eyes which appear slanted
4. Single transverse crease across a flabby, limp hand
5. Inward curving little finger
6. Nose with flat bridge and upturned nostrils
7. Fused ear lobules
8. Deep cleft between big toe and second toe
9. Small flattened skull
10. Short fifth finger
11. Smooth, simple outer ear lobe
12. Congenital heart problem
13. Little fingers with one crease instead of two[*]

Unfortunately, in order to aid early diagnosis, these physical characteristics don't always show themselves at birth and can only be noticed later in the child's development. In Adam's case, some of them manifested themselves only gradually. As a result, only a chromosomal karyotype test after birth yields a definitive diagnosis. In the case of pre-birth, an amniocentesis test identifies the condition of Down syndrome in the fetus

Before going forward, to ensure that everyone understands what a syndrome entails, it might be helpful to cite Merriam-Webster's Dictionary definition of syndrome as "a group of signs and symptoms that occur together and characterize a particular abnormality or condition".[*]

In Adam's case, it was the nurse who assisted with the birth who was the first one to notice the crease (cf. No.4) across the middle of Adam's small hand. She reluctantly told me of her concern as I looked into the eyes of my newborn for the first time that early April 2nd morning. She indicated that she had reservations, though, because Adam had that crease on only one hand and, according to her, he looked "so cute". Other than that, there were initially no other outward signs that our son had Down Syndrome. I decided not to tell Barb until she was out of the hospital.

Barb and I eventually learned that few Downs have all of these physical features and that there are, surprisingly, people who have some of these signs but do not have this condition. Consequently, it would have been malpractice for any health care worker to make any immediate diagnosis during those few days after our son's birth. Adam's pediatrician could only add that our little guy's overall body seemed "floppy". It took six agonizing weeks to confirm the syndrome's existence in our son's tiny, fragile body. It took even more out of us emotionally to wait to see if Adam fit into that cruel statistic that he was that one out of 700 births with Down syndrome.

One thing that all the doctors and scientists can agree upon is that they do not know the cause of Down syndrome. It is a genetic anomaly caused by an extra copy of the 21st chromosome, hence the term Trisomy twenty-one". In spite of the fact that *Tri* means three, my more positive-thinking, half-Irish wife, decided to call Adam our "4-Leaf Clover", a symbol of good luck. We both eventually discovered that the difference between ordinary and "extraordinary" is just that little extra which turned out to be love, understanding, help, prodding and praying. When it came to any challenges, Adam's mother likes to accent the positive, reflected by the lyrics of the Nitty Gritty Dirt Band: ☒"If we're ever going to see a rainbow, we've got to stand a little rain" * According to Irish mythology, there will be a pot of gold at the end of that rainbow and, using that metaphor, our lives are indeed, enriched by Adam.

Not knowing the cause of Down syndrome, paradoxically, would be a blessing in that it meant that no one was to blame. After having raised two older children already, Barb and I knew that it was counterproductive to play the blame-game. Too many marriages have been destroyed by this unfair game. When life happens, effective. Even when disciplining our kids Barb and I presented a united front and discuss any differences we might have had, when our kids weren't around. We learned that when adversity hits, don't ask "who's responsible?" but take the steps to respond. Actions have consequences and, in our case, they produce positive results.

1. Daughter Angela, son Jeff, and my beautiful wife Barbara, 7 months pregnant

The photo above is worth a thousand words when I notice the joy on my children's faces and the "glow" on Barbara's countenance. In some respects the cliche "ignorance is bliss" applies here because Barbara did not have an amniocentesis test. Had we asked for one, we would have found out that our unborn child had Down syndrome. That would have prolonged our denial, disbelief, grief and sorrow. Or, it might have given us more time to prepare and accept the diagnosis. At any rate, Adam was going to be given all the love he deserved. But, first I wanted to make sure ignorance on our part would not hinder our infant son's physical and emotional growth.

As a former teacher of 35 years, I knew where to look for the answers. I eventually found them talking to doctors and psychologists, reading books and articles on Down syndrome, and seeking out parents with cognitively disabled children and organizations that helped parents with special needs children like Adam. I made sure I shared all the information with Barb and she made sure that I treated Adam more as a son and less as a subject.

One of the objectives, then, of this book is to educate and comfort those who are facing the challenges associated with an exceptional child; to learn how to be "acceptional" and to give hope by using some of the proven approaches, which make it easier on the child as well as the parents. I am certainly not a doctor, and maybe some of my information and observations might be outdated, but whatever knowledge I acquired about Down syndrome, we used with our son, especially when it came to many of the remediation strategies. Adam is proof that most of them helped. I'm paraphrasing the American poet Robert Frost who maintained that intelligence is not necessarily the accumulation of knowledge and facts, but what is done with them. We made sure to use the recommendations of the experts. The axiom "knowledge is power" was definitely pertinent here.

Nonetheless, unlike intellect, wisdom comes from experience, which is the best teacher. With the printing of this book, My wife and I have had 43 years of that experience living with Adam. Hopefully, with that reality, we will be able to offer comfort as well as guidance to the reader. The authorship of this quote is lost in history but not to our ability to relate: "I will not judge another man until I have walked a mile in his shoes". And to bring that proverb more up to date we can aver that that we have walked the walk. Not to sugarcoat our own situation, ours was fraught with anxiety and some missteps and we also went through stages similar to those that people experience with loss. Hopefully, the following chapters will shed some light on what we went through but how we overcame them. The following are the stages we went through:

Stage 1: **Disbelief** along with denial

Stage 2: **Grief** and sorrow
Stage 3: **Hope** strengthened by faith
Stage 4: **Awareness** through education
Stage 5: **Respite** and well-being

I have devoted a chapter for each one of these stages because they deserve the attention in order to make things easier on parents and more helpful for their child. I do not want to skim over anything and hopefully will provide enough information, I realize that all children are different, and that also applies to Downs kids. Yet, quite a number of the proposed strategies in this book are applicable to many of them.

STAGE 1

DISBELIEF ✤

"That which is denied cannot be healed"~ Brennan Manning *

"Your son has tested positive for Downs syndrome," said the pediatrician matter-of-factly on the other end of the phone line. I was standing at that tense time outside the principal's office on a public phone in the hallway of John Marshall High School. My wife and I had spent many days dreading the diagnosis from the clinicians at our capital in Madison. It had been an agonizing six weeks and those words now were seared into my brain. How could this be?

While I was still on the phone with the pediatrician, stunned by this information, all I could distinguish further in the conversation were words like "drooling, severely retarded, early passing, should be institutionalized. Well, maybe I better back up."

I responded emphatically, "Yes, you had better! We are not going to put our son in an institution and that's final. You are going to help us understand what we need to do to keep him at home."

No child deserves abandonment but, rather, an even more involvement in a loving and engaging environment. As an experienced educator, I knew that children thrive if given attention and love. So, Adam was a keeper. Yet, the disbelief in the diagnosis continued to gnaw away at my heart and soul.

I had already put in ten years at Marshall and thought I had the world by the arse. Barbara and I had recently purchased our first home and our first new car. I was given an excellent rating on my teacher evaluation form. I felt like I was a really great teacher. Maybe it was too much hubris which made God decide that since I thought I was such an outstanding teacher, "O.K. smarty pants, take care of one of My special children." Or just possibly, because I was a teacher, I had the necessary skills to raise a special child?

The world now seemed particularly cruel and unforgiving. Barb and I felt that it was a cruel twist of fate that my sister Kathy gave birth to a perfectly healthy boy only nine days later. Here was the conundrum, though. If I believed it was just fate, that meant I didn't have a choice. My faith told me, though, God gives us free will. So, instead of fate, I concluded that we must follow the precepts of divine intervention and help "one of God's children".

It was a real punch in the gut as I look back on that morning on April 2nd with that revelation, dazed, and standing all by myself in the maternity ward. I was hoping against hope that the nurse and doctors would be eventually proven wrong. I couldn't bring myself to tell Barb about the prognosis and cause her more emotional anguish. There was the physical pain Barbara was already experiencing by spending extra days in the hospital recuperating from a tubal ligation. Of course, the irony did not escape me. As a result, I did not want to reveal to her what the nurse had feared. I was still numb with disbelief myself.

With one exception, I spent the first three days in solitary sadness at home and at work. I was able to share my worst fears with a colleague at school. Sobbing and shaking, I stood there in the foyer revealing my deep sorrow. The only consolation she could give me was that, in all likelihood. Adam did not have Down syndrome. She was mercifully saved by the passing bell. I had to return to my classroom pretending that there was nothing wrong.

It took Barb and I several weeks after the diagnosis to tell our parents and other family members about Adam's condition. Our nine-year-old daughter Angela was just happy that she now had a baby brother she always wanted and was unaware of the challenges ahead. Angie got the live doll she wanted so badly. She later confessed to me that she told Barb to "sneak in" a baby for her...Heeeeerrre's Adam!

As for our 13-year-old son Jeff, he was more concerned with the uncertainties which plague all 13-year-olds. He did, however, agree to help out as much as he could with his baby brother. We knew that Jeff loved his brother and became protective of him as both grew older. He shared a bedroom with Adam who used to groan while gnawing on his thumb every night. Jeff never complained even though he had to wake Adam to remind him to lie down and go back to sleep.

2. Brother Jeff and sister Angela (not the nun) with papoose Adam

3

Maybe it was due to denial, even though we were told that early intervention was the key for any child with Adam's condition, we wanted to forego the therapy and doctor visits for the time being. The poking and prodding would have to wait until we were satisfied with hugging, bathing, and snuggling with our newborn. We also decided not to tell our parents, relatives, or friends. Was this procrastination due to denial or was it shame which kept us from telling others? Were there still vestiges of disbelief? Or was it that we didn't want others to feel our disappointment? During those first six weeks, we might have still wished that the doctors were wrong and that we should wait. It is safe to say that the byproduct of disbelief is doubt. That doubt hung like a cloud over our heads those heart-rending weeks. Nonetheless, if the first picture of Adam in this book is any indication of denial, it certainly is a portrait of a Down syndrome child.

I was aware that Barb had prayed for a third child but did not know, at first, that God had granted her that wish. If that child was not exactly what she had prayed for, she remained staunch that his special needs would be given the best maternal care she could muster. She was ADAMant that, "Everyone has a right to live on this planet." Her belief in unconditional love has been a major facet of her value system. In contrast, my love sometimes was more transactional. I remember telling her that we already had two healthy children and that we were pushing our luck. She indicated that she was 34, but still had an abundance of love to give. I have always wished to be as selfless and loving as she is. I'm reminded of the old Jewish proverb: "God could not be everywhere, so He created mothers".

After our son Jeff was born, she gave up smoking because she didn't want to handle a newborn with dirty fingers or kiss him with a smoky breath. It took an angioplasty years later for me to quit the habit. When our daughter Angela was born, Barb made sure that her daughter had clean clothes and combed hair from infancy on. There were those constantly available loving and gentle hands that worked their wonders as she cared for all of us. Without a doubt, Adam was going to be in good hands. I made sure to tell her how I envied her ability to love unconditionally. To this day, I am fortunate to have her as my role model.

With few exceptions, we used the same parenting practices on Adam as we did with his siblings. Jeff and Angela were happy and well-adjusted kids; a great source of pride for us. Patience and consistency, mixed in with love, had proven to be a good formula for raising children. Of course, our parenting was forever a work in progress and one which required constant mindfulness.

Adam's siblings became eager tutors who helped with his social and lifetime skills. They treated him with patience and showed happiness for any and all of his successes. The reading, writing, and 'rithmatic came later in the special education classes at the schools he attended. It is safe to say that Adam's livelihood and education was a group effort. I know that maybe "it takes a whole village" is a cliche, but in our family's case, it was a fact.

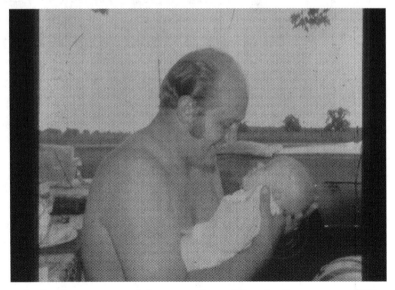

3. A quiet moment with my newborn Adam in the summer of '78

Eventually, our parents came around also to the same hopeful outlook as ours for Adam. He was developing particularly well and meeting the yearly expectations for a child. His physical growth was what was expected and he was not that far behind with crawling, walking, and talking. We were fortunate that we already had two other children, who could help us with Adam's development and needs. In addition, they were tremendously important as babysitters. However, the most significant advantage we had over other parents is that we knew what those milestones looked like when our other two older kids were growing up. To help the entire household, Barb decided to do child care to supplement our income and to stay at home with Adam. This was beneficial in two extra ways: Barb learned more about rearing children while Adam had home-companions to play with.

When Adam was six, a colleague of mine suggested I apply for a temporary license to teach special education classes and thereby help Adam even more by applying more remediation strategies. I decided to take some graduate classes at Cardinal Stritch College for the license. After learning how challenging it was to teach special education classes and that some of these teachers experienced burn-out after an average of seven years, I changed my mind about taking on an entirely new curriculum. In little time I discovered how large a chasm there was between advanced Latin classes and the special ed classroom. However, I did not regret taking those graduate classes because they made me a better teacher in my Latin and English classes.

In hindsight, I believe Barb would have been a much better candidate for that license than I because she was already providing her own special education classes for Adam, in-home. Her teaching did not involve any textbooks or professor however--just a mother's love and true understanding.

STAGE 2

GRIEF ✿

"Those who do not weep, do not see" * ~ Victor Hugo

The second punch to the gut came shortly after Adam's Down syndrome diagnosis. It was his pediatrician who told us that he had heard a heart murmur and our baby would need to visit a cardiologist. We already knew and feared the fact that some Downs had heart defects. One week later we were told by the pediatric cardiologist that Adam did, in fact, have a hole in his heart. The first six weeks had already been broken up with tears and fears, not so much for ourselves but more for Adam. Now we had this to deal with.

With that news, Barb and I were left with an even larger hole in our hearts. This diagnosis was going to test our faith in God. I wondered how God could give our beautiful boy such a life sentence. However, in a weird way, his heart condition gave us reprieve from concern about the Down syndrome and we focused more on his heart health. This was just another reason Barb and I didn't want to do any more doctor visits or early intervention strategies in the first place. Now we only wanted to enjoy as much carefree time with our baby just in case our time with him would be cut short. Yet, the tearful days and nights still lingered. We had never known such sorrow before.

Since our infant Adam didn't have all the features of a Downs yet, we wondered whether he could have fooled my parents, relatives, and good friends who came to visit in the ensuing weeks. Even his godparents, Karen and Eddie, were unaware of Adam's condition six weeks later at his baptism. We found this out the hard way because they were very disappointed that we didn't have enough faith in them to tell them. In hindsight, they might have even offered us some solace.

Still there were those nagging questions. Was it shame which kept us from revealing to others what we now knew to be the truth? Were we afraid that others would feel the disappointment more than we did?. Would there be whispers or awkward moments from people we knew so well? How would our kids react to the news that their brother was retarded? Would they feel any shame being seen with him in public? Were we the ones who were weak-minded? These were the many questions that would need answering before we could continue with our family life. The following weeks would provide all the answers

Because Adam's life was so fragile now, Barb and I decided we needed the support of our immediate family. We had suffered alone long enough. We started to sense that it was a big mistake when we chose not to tell them. It was now time.

I vividly recall my visit to my parent's home for the first time. My father was still at work and my mother was busy making supper. I needed to unburden myself and hoped my mother would help me with the emotional load I was carrying. I first hesitated and then choked on my words as I told her about Adam. Her tears flowed profusely as she kept whimpering "Poor baby, poor baby!" Just saying it: "Adam has Down syndrome and a hole in his heart" was even more painful because I now felt the stark reality of what I was hearing. As I held back my tears, I tried to console my mother with the assurance that Adam was under the best of care, and that we would just have to pray for the strength to carry on and help Adam get better by taking a more proactive role with his challenges.

Whereas my father was in the first stage of denial, my mother's emotions were raw with sorrow. After he finally heard the news, he was sympathetic but hid his disappointment by reassuring himself with "Oh, don't worry, he will grow out of it". I didn't bother to correct him

We quickly discovered that our parents, family members and friends took the cue from us by the way we showed more confidence and less remorse. They acted in kind, figuring that they did not have to commiserate with us because we didn't cry or say "woe is me". We finally had more moral support from caring people. Our cheerfulness and more positive outlook now trumped any misgivings they might have had about how we handled our own grief.

I present a scenario as an example: let's say, your child falls down onto the floor and he looks up to you for your reaction. If you calmly tell your toddler, "That's alright, let me see your boo-boo". In all likelihood, there will be no drama, However, if you gasp or show alarm, you can expect a lot of crying and crocodile tears. My Dad was especially good at this ruse. When Adam was a toddler he would sometimes fall on the living room carpet. Before Adam could start crying, grandpa would tell him from the comfort of his easy chair, "Come here, and I will pick you up." I was always delighted at that calm, tricky distraction, which kept Adam from any disconcerting scenario.

Our parent's final lesson, after all those years, was that they learned how to demonstrate tenderness. My dad learned "by heart" how to show affection toward his grandchildren, the kind we were never recipients of when we were their age. I honestly believe, to this day, my father learned how to show compassion for his grandchildren by observing us.

As weeks went by, I watched with admiration how Barb interacted with Adam. She treated him like she treated our first two children. In the evenings, he would spend time on his baby blanket on the floor while we watched television. Jeff and Angie would be down on the floor with him, talking and playing while Adam's eyes would be open with wonderment. Barb would pick him up just before bedtime every evening and snuggle with him. Then she would take him upstairs and place him in his crib and stroke his head lovingly. Adam was not going to be hidden in some far off room. He was not going to be treated like an invalid or a recluse. The only drooling came as a result of his gurgling and cooing.

I remember watching a documentary film years ago where behavioral scientists at Oxford University did an experiment to find out what happens to a person when denied prolonged stimulation. They placed the trial subject in a dark room floating in a water-filled vat. That person was locked in this flotation tank for a week to discover what happens with prolonged sensory deprivation By the 6ᵗʰ or 7ᵗʰ day, that individual was stark raving mad.

I wish I could remember the name of this same documentary where a scientist was placed in a igloo-like structure in Antarctica with no light, no sound, nothing to stimulate any of his senses, only food and water in this kind of solitary confinement. He was rescued about two weeks later. He was heard babbling about seeing angels and other strange encounters.

There was also a 1980 fiction film, "Altered States", which also featured a flotation tank and a scientist played by William Hurt who subjected himself to a similar experiment. Even though the results of these experiments were more dramatically provocative, it did show how human touch and voice are critical to a person's psychological health.

I recently found a few online articles which corroborates all my own suspicions:

"**Research** demonstrates that **touch** contains several health benefits for our psychological and physiological well being...

According to the research conducted at the University of North Carolina, women who receive more hugs from their partners have lower heart rates and blood pressure and higher levels of oxytocin…" * Jul 8, 2018

In an another article titled "The Surprising Value of Human Touch", by Lauren Suval, the author confirmed what research has found to be consequential: "Whenever I'm overwhelmed or feeling down, I crave a touch, a hug to hold; a connection that can manifest into something that's tangible…even on stress-free days, I may seek out the healing components that touch has to offer… Hugging induces Oxytocin, the "bonding hormone", renowned for reducing stress, lowering cortisol levels and increasing a sense of trust and security". *

4. Adam getting a much-needed hug from
Mom and Curious George

STAGE 3

HOPE ❧

"Hope is stronger than fear" * ~Buddha quote

The birth of a child with Down syndrome raises special problems. Our own parenting skills were going to be put to the test. In spite of that, it isn't necessarily the great tragedy for the family that the child is born into. With proper support in the early, formative years and, later, help from day centers or special education classes in public schools, those efforts will produce results. Barb and I found that the rearing of a Down syndrome child need not handicap a rewarding experience. We became aware that patience and understanding are both necessary and helpful tools for rearing our child. These efforts also transferred from us to our other children as well.

As I pointed out earlier that "it takes a village to raise a child" can be a cliche, but in the case of helping a mentally challenged child, it takes on even more validity. Since Barb and I agreed that we would never institutionalize Adam as one of the physicians recommended, we decided on early intervention as the alternative. There were many neighborhood organizations and groups which would make a significant difference in helping with the task of raising a special child. In addition to the support, they could give helpful advice to make it easier on the parent as well as the child. I am so glad we sought their help, which gave us valuable coping skills as well.

Shortly after six weeks Sarilee Maney, March of Dimes National Nurse of the Year not only helped Adam, but also gave us much-needed advice. Sarah came to our home twice a week for about six months to give Adam physical and occupational therapy. She had been working out of the Children's Hospital in Milwaukee. In addition to working with Adam, she also gave us guidance and was especially instrumental with giving us the hope and assurances that Adam would do well in his future endeavors. In hindsight it was nurses who played a major role in our child's health in addition to his mental and physical development. Jumping ahead 42 years during that awful pandemic in 2020, then president-elect Joe Biden made an interesting observation that "Doctors let you live, nurses make you want to live. If there are any angels in heaven, they are nurses" Oct.19, 2020 *

"It's a Miracle!" exclaimed the pediatric cardiologist at Children's Hospital. With a broad smile on his face, he told us that Adam's hole in the heart had miraculously disappeared. Here's were "retarded" would be an operative word because it comes from the Latin adjective "tardus" which means slow. In Adam's case, I firmly feel that the heart was just a little slower in becoming fully developed. Just before we left the office a beaming doctor announced, "See, I don't always bring bad news".

After the wonderful news about Adam's heart we lived the first three years with guarded optimism. However, the first 10 years Adam survived Wisconsin winters on a steady course of Amoxicillin due to his weak lungs and immune system, which also turned out to be slower in their development. In the months after the flu season we paid more attention to Adam's psychological needs.

We didn't pay as much attention to Adam's IQ as to his emotional intelligence or EQ (Emotional Quotient) because I genuinely felt that attitude is more important than aptitude as more of a measure for future success. With IQs, parents' expectations can be higher or lower depending upon the score and therefore fewer children are challenged and less is expected of them. We set Adam up for success by expecting more from him without pushing him unrealistically. As a teacher, I knew that the average IQ was 100 on that bell curve with the majority of people falling somewhere between 85 and 115. A person is considered retarded if he or she has an IQ of less than 70. Adam scored a bit lower than that 70 range. Barb and I figured we could work with that. Inaction was not an option.

In spite of all the intellectual obstacles our Adam had to overcome, he excelled in social IQ or EQ. Emotional intelligence is the ability to understand, use, and manage our own emotions in positive ways to relieve stress, communicate effectively, empathize with others, overcome challenges and defuse conflict. I have consistently maintained that self-awareness plays a major role in EQ.

We, naturally, were inquisitive about Adam's IQ at first because I had read somewhere that in addition to Trisomy-21, there was a condition called mosaicism which resulted in a higher IQ average for the Downs child. Adam had a chromosome test done at St. Joseph's Hospital and received a report that mosaicism could not be ruled out. This gave us some hope until I called Dr. June Dobbs, expert on Trisomy-21 and mosaicism. She stopped me before I could continue my questioning and informed me that there really was not that much of a difference between a mosaic or the classic Trisomy-21 in terms of intellectual capabilities. I remember her insistence and abrupt comment, 'Mosaic-schmozaic!' The reason Adam is doing so well is because of the early intervention program you have him on".

Barb and I had been told that early intervention was the perfect approach to help Adam along his long journey into maturity and good health. I had learned much later from a professor at Cardinal Stritch in a graduate Special Education class that if we take an ordinary child and keep him or her in a room and ignored in their early formative year, they will also exhibit signs of retardation. She called this lack of proper parenting "cultural-familial retardation" when compared to "clinical retardation", as exhibited by children like Adam who are born with physical and/or physiological anomalies.

That class at Cardinal Stritch was taken in 1984. Since then, I have found out that the definition of familial retardation has not changed much, but better defined in a recent research which I found online:

"Familial Retardation, also called socio-cultural or cultural-familial retardation, refers to a state of mild mental retardation that is believed to be the result of environmental factors, usually related to some types of psychosocial disadvantages; lack of parental care, impoverished circumstances, poor diet, lack of intellectual stimulation, and opportunity, etc. rather than an identifiable physiological or neurological reason. This type of retardation, generally noted as an all-around slowness is not usually noted prior to a child starting school" *

It should be noted that the term "retardation" is still being used today and is not considered as a pejorative by Barb, me, and even Adam. There are some who feel that the word should not be used and they are entitled to their feelings. Yet, "retarded" was so commonly used by professionals and others in our community, Barbara and I didn't find it necesary to use a euphemism for Adam's condition. Our retarded son continued to be treated with affection and understanding.

Here is more information I found online recently in my research of retardation:

"In 1995, an Atlanta study conducted jointly by the Centers for Disease Control and Prevention and Emory University found important new evidence linking mild retardation to social and educational deprivation. It was found that 8.4 our of every 1,000 10-year-olds were mildly retarded (defined as an IQ of 50-70), while 3.6 of every 1,000 10-year-olds suffered severe retardation due to conditions as cerebral palsy or **Down Syndrome**". *

I found this intriguing because I can still remember my professor fearing that, unless the educational needs of more of our students are met, cultural- familial retardation would double in the 21st Century. This professor did not have prophetic powers, just like I didn't in my classes when I predicted that students who didn't do their homework would fail. At the minimum, it was just sage advice.

Since those important formative years are between the ages of 0 to 6, as an educator, I certainly knew how critical proper parenting can be. I'd already seen the negative results of bad parenting of the so-called "normal" child. It was, therefore, crucial that an exceptional child get exceptional care early if we wanted our child to be a productive member of society.

My professor told us educators that, unlike clinical retardation, cultural retardation can be cured. The following was a study that really hits home:

"Familial retardation may be reduced by nutritional, health, and educational intervention at an early age. In a study conducted in the 1970s, educators selected mother-child pairs from among a group of women with IQs under 75 living in the poorest section of **Milwaukee, Wisconsin,** while establishing a **control group** of mothers in the same neighborhood with IQs over 100. For the first five years of the children's lives, the targeted group of mothers and their children received instruction in problem-solving and language skills, as well as counseling to motivate them to learn and succeed. The mothers and children in the control group received no form of environmental enrichment. At the age of five, the children in the target group had IQ scores averaging 26 points higher than those of the children in the control group. At the age of nine, their average IQ was 106 (slightly above the universal **norm** of 100), while that of the other children was only 79". *

Before continuing, I need to remind everyone how the public school system, including Milwaukee's, sees to the "nutritional, health, and educational intervention" for its students by providing breakfast, and lunch programs, by providing all kinds of health screenings, and by offering classes that address the needs of students like Adam with special education classes.

No one can argue about the significance of the Intelligence Quotient (IQ), which is one of the tools we use to measure aptitude. Yet, I've constantly told my high school students that, yes, **aptitude** is great, but that **attitude** is greater. Especially for success in social settings like the workforce. In my teaching experience I have seen how disruptive students with bad attitudes will affect the classroom and their grades, That being said, if Adam was not going to be an Einstein, Barbara and I aimed to make him more like a Helen Keller. If eyes are the windows to the soul, the glint in our baby Adam's eyes was so reassuring and convincing. That glint with that sweet smile told me, "It's all going to be OK... It's all going to be OK"

5. Adam (on the left) with cousin Philip on their 1st birthdays

Those special education classes at Stritch helped me understand Adam better and how helpful my wife's handling of his needs were. As I reflect on those classes, I can say with certainty that they made me not only a better father but also a better teacher. The most significant thing I learned was that just because it was clear and understandable to me didn't mean that it was evident to my students because they had different learning styles and came into my classroom with different life experiences. I also learned that my students didn't care how much I know but wanted to know how much I care.

In every sense of the word, education is the great equalizer. Knowledge is power and we wanted to make Adam more knowledgeable so that he would be more independent. I had heard somewhere that educated people are easy to rule but impossible to enslave. We realized that it would take a lot of patience and perseverance for this to become a reality. So, I am reminded by a quote from the great dancer/actor Eddie Cantor: "It took me 20 years to become an overnight success." *

As with my students, I always explained why learning something was important or necessary not just "because I said so". Giving them a reason made them more receptive to the task. The explanation showed understanding and willingness to work with them.

I also came to the realization that children respond better to praise than to criticism. Kids are continually starved for reassurance and validation. I learned this from coaching high school boys and girls. This applies even more to the youngsters. It is so much easier to criticize them than to correct them. It makes more sense to build them up as a child than to lock them up as an adult. The sage Dalia Lama proposed that "Our prime purpose in this life is to help others. And if you can't help them, at least don't hurt them". * Not enough can be said about this sage advice.

While Adam was responding well to all of the early intervention strategies, Barb decided to do child care to help with finances after leaving her employment as a nurse's aide. A fringe benefit for Adam was now he had playmates his age, who would challenge him by learning how to interact and play with them.

On most days TV was a boon tube and not the boob tube for Adam because he learned so much watching his favorite program, Sesame Street. Adam was fond of all the characters, but was particularly impressed with the Count. He was intrigued by the numbers, and, unfortunately still is today, even though math is not his strong suit. His godmother, Karen Horwath, was really adept at knitting and made for him Big Bird who accompanied him to bed every night.

Mr. Rogers was such a wonderful TV role model with his friendly smile, and even more wonderful advice for social situations. It can't be emphasized enough what he did for the viewers' self-esteem. He made Adam feel good about himself.

Adam, like other kids his age, was also entertained by the Muppets. He laughed at the interaction between Miss Piggy and Kermit. In addition to the TV shows, he would watch the VHS tapes featuring the entire Muppet crew where he also learned all of the songs.

For some reason, Adam still enjoys watching soap operas. I kid him frequently by renaming his favorites -- "As Your Stomach Turns" and "The Old and the Senseless". He also watches the old sitcoms from the 60s and 70s. He got many belly laughs out of "I Love Lucy". Adam still likes to laugh and watches the older sitcoms in his new bedroom in our new house.

STAGE 4

AWARENESS ♣

"What is necessary to change a person is to change
his awareness of himself."*~Abraham Maslow

"Know thyself" is an old Greek axiom, and words I learned to
live by. I already knew that there are three levels of consciousness
as described by Dr. Sigmund Freud: the id, ego, and superego,
Simply put, the id is our subconscious, the ego is the conscious,
and the superego is our conscience. More importantly though,
I discovered that all people possess three personas: The person
other people think we are, the person we think we are, and most
importantly, the person we really are. That last one will keep us
out of a heap of trouble...if we know ourselves.

We can all appreciate the need for an informed and intelligent
population and their obvious contributions to society. However,
there are instances where some of these people are more smart
than they are understanding. For instance, a chemist knows what
kind of reaction he will get when he mixes A with B, but then can't
understand why his wife wants a divorce because he constantly
mocks her. We should all be familiar with the archetypes of the

mad scientist or the absent-minded professor in literature and screen plays. Both are shown to lack a certain EQ.

As a teacher I saw how socially inept some of my very bright students were. Those who were narcissistic and impatient with other students made themselves extremely unpopular and social outcasts. Because some of them were so critical of others, I feared that they would not get along with their fellow employees, unless they were the boss. They should have been aware that one's disposition is just as important as position. And we know what employees think of some of their bosses. This might seem to be an oversimplification, but self-awareness in each of these parties would make life easier for all of them.

I also observed how many of my students of varying skill levels adapted quite well in a classroom setting. Their personal skills added to the enjoyment of the class by their attitude towards their peers. In my English and German classes they all knew that kindness was a language deaf people can hear and the blind can see. A smile always begets a smile. Our faces are like mirrors and frowns will never make another person smile.

When I was taking my post graduate classes in exceptional education at Cardinal Stritch College in 1984, the most relevant thing I learned was that there were three environments that were crucial in determining a child's mental health. Those three were how the child functioned at home, in school, and in public. Problems in two of these areas require that the child would need remediation. That social IQ, as the professor called it, was critical for that person's ability to have future success in society. I prefer to call the social IQ "attitude" and the mental IQ "aptitude".

Even at the age of three, Adam delighted in being at social settings, whether with family or out at a restaurant or at school. His "please" and "thank you" always drew smiles. His pleasant demeanor and beaming face delighted everyone in the room. At the age of three, he was already winning hearts as the 1981 Easter Seal Poster Child. His TV appearances made us so proud and pleased Easter Seals so much because he would entertain the TV hosts with his bubbly personality. At that point we became aware that Adam's future looked brighter because he was already extraordinary in all those three social settings I touched upon earlier. As I reflected on my son's progress, I noticed that Adam had that little "extra" in "extraordinary", and Barb and I have made sure that he was aware of that.

6. *Adam, seated with Easter Seal Ambassador Pat Thomas, with Emmett Prosser who was the 1981 co-poster child for Easter Seal.*

But don't take my word for it. When Adam was only 10, and we were visiting the home of my mentor and colleague, Elaine Steiger, she noted: "You know, Adam is more articulate and intelligent than some of my Latin students".

"I think we have to give Adam more credit for his successes also", according to my wife, and especially when it comes to his personality. Lloyd M Dunn editor of *Exceptional Education in Transition* * says, "Research has somewhat dispelled the stereotype that all Downs syndrome children are cheerful, affectionate and docile although Johnson and Abelson (1969) found such children to have a greater social competence than other retardates of comparable intelligence. Wunsch (1957) found that many are happy and lovable, especially when young, but others are aggressive and hostile, particularly those who reached adolescence and adulthood...Nevertheless, Downs children as a group fit in better at home and in the community than do retarded children with organic brain injury". *

With these considerations in mind, I need to explain that this is research I came across when Adam was quite young and the information above is easily more than almost 50 years old. As a matter of fact, the scientific community has not observed much changes with personality profiles since then. After 42 years of living with Adam, the more common stereotypes of cheerfulness, affection, and docility still apply to him.

In a more recent online article *, "The emergence of a syndrome-specific personality profile in young children", written by Deborah Fidler, she affirms what the scientific community said years ago about children with this syndrome:

"For decades, researchers and practitioners have attempted to describe commonalities in personality style among individuals with Down Syndrome, with some arguing for a stereotype involving a pleasant, affectionate, and passive personality (Gibbs & Thorpe, 1983; Rodgers, 1987). This stereotype had been supported by studies of parent perception of children with Down syndrome, where in one study, over 50% of 11 year old children with Down syndrome were described as "affectionate", "lovable" and "getting on well with other people", and "fun" (Carr 1995). There are also reports of increased positive mood and predictability in behavior in individuals with Down syndrome, supporting the more positive pleasant aspects of personality stereotype, as well as reports of lower activity levels, less persistence, and distractibility than other children, supporting the more passive aspects of the stereotype (Gunn & Cuskely, 1991).

"However...In addition to these positive perceptions of personality in individuals with Down syndrome, other research reports have described individuals with Down syndrome as showing a specific motivational orientation involving lower levels of task persistence and higher levels of off-task social behaviors. This lowered persistence is sometimes complemented by a stubborn or strong willed personality streak, also described in studies of temperament in Down syndrome. (Carr, 1995; Gibson 1978)."*

If the last sentence in this article is correct, Barbara and I are more than happy to put up with these human foibles which every parent must admit shows up in "normal" children.

7. Enjoying his life as a happy three-year-old

STAGE 5

RESPITE ♣

"If you are depressed, you are living in the past
If you are anxious, you are living in the future
If you are at peace, you are living in the present"* ~Lao Tzu

I need to point out that not everyone goes through all of these five stages and they sometimes overlap or regress. What Barb and I did know was that not doing anything was worse than making that occasional mistake. We were not afraid to go forward because parents are not perfect. We practised patience because we had reminded myself to "Behold the turtle: it makes progress only when it sticks its neck out". * We determined that parenting is less of a science, but more an art. We realized that it is a persistent work in progress and, therefore, we never stop being parents.

Later on, as the nest gets empty, we still keep an eye on our children's nest. I truly believe that parents can see how well they raised their children by how they bring up their own. In our case, we never had an empty nest because Adam still lives with us today. Yet, we have no complaints because Barb and I had ample help with any successes we might have had with Adam in the past 43 years. We have come to realize that nobody can succeed alone, even more so with an exceptional person. I believe that those of us who are more capable have the obligation to care for those who are handicapable. To Adam's benefit., those obligations were met by numerous people and organizations.

I have already indicated how nurse Sarah Maney helped us with Adam's physical challenges. Doctors at Children's Hospital were always available for advice and care. I recall how I contacted a Down syndrome specialist there after I read somewhere that there was a chance that Adam had a "mosaic" chromosome instead of the common Trisomy 21. This specific chromosome promised a child with a higher IQ. We were informed that the reason Adam was doing so well was because of the early intervention strategies.

When Adam was about a year old, visiting nurse Sarilee Maney suggested we send Adam to Easter Seals classes because they could continue better with his early intervention. His success in those morning classes(which we were able to view through a one-way mirror.) were so pronounced that he was chosen as a poster child in 1981. All-in-all, everyone was impressed with his greatest asset, which was his politeness. "Thank you" and "please" were the best examples.

Because the Milwaukee Public Schools were required by state law to allow Adam into special education classes at their pre-school sites, he attended Grant Grade School. Adam did so well, increasing his vocabulary by leaps and bounds and was "a pleasure to work with" according to his teachers".

I've already mentioned that education is the real equalizer. And, thank God for public schools! Sadly, if we would have had to depend on private schools, Adam would not have gotten the quality education he was entitled to. I find it ironic that private schools preach, "Suffer little children to come unto me" but then follow up silently with "as long as there is nothing wrong with them."

To further aid Adam with his physical and social needs, Special Olympics stepped in and gave him the opportunity to excel in other areas of his development. He would beam with joy and pride whenever we took photos of him with his medals and ribbons as he stood on the winners stands. He even made it to the finals of the Special Olympics which were held in Stevens Point, Wisconsin each year. It was a weekend event which required our little qualifier to spend the night in a college dorm. We were afraid that he would miss us too much. No worry! Adam actually preferred sharing a room with his fellow athletes.

At that meet one year, Adam had qualified in the 100 meter dash. After the starter's gun went off, all eight of the runners were making their way to the finish line. Adam fell behind while the leader was being cheered on by the enthusiastic crowd of parents sitting in the stands. Then, the little speedster stopped 10 meters short of the finish tape, faced the stands, and waved to his fans while the others ran past him. Adam took a third place ribbon as a result of the leader's need to show his appreciation to his adoring crowd. Now, that was "special"!

As a high school track coach at that time, I was thrilled to see how these selfless athletes enjoyed the opportunity to compete in their own special way. The WIAA High School Track and Field State Meet was being held that same weekend at the state capital in Madison. Marshall's Boys Track Team had several qualifiers. One of our jumpers was in a good position to take first place. As soon as he took his final jump, I knew that he was the state champion. However, this gifted athlete didn't reflect the same attitude and work ethic as the special Olympians did. I was somewhat happy for him, congratulated him, and asked my jump coach to take charge to get the athletes home on the school bus without me. Then, I immediately drove to Stevens Point to join my wife to watch Adam compete.

We don't remember what kind of ribbons Adam won in the other events he had qualified for. All we remember are the smiles and the high-fives he got from me, his Mom, and his fellow special olympians. As a coach, I knew what it was like to be competitive and what winning meant. In the case of our Adam the look of satisfaction on his face made him a winner in the truest sense.

On the long rides back to Milwaukee, Adam would insist we stop at a McDonalds for a quarter pounder with fries. After this "happy" meal, he would go into a food coma and sleep the rest of the way home.

Whenever we were at home, Adam also participated in Special Olympics bowling leagues. He loved to hear the sound of the pins falling under the weight of the bowling balls. He enjoyed doing the high-fives with his friends, which were followed by every round. With the help of guard rails, every shot at the pins was met with success. The only hazard was whenever someone forgot to release the ball soon enough and ended with a loud thump!

8. In the stands at the Special Olympics State Meet

Lions Club gave Adam the camping experience while we were able to get some respite when he had those week-long overnighters at locations in northern Wisconsin. We were still worried whether he would miss us too much. Our worries were unfounded. He was mister independent now.

High School offered Adam even more independence and great teachers at Hamilton High. It was there that he teamed up with special ed teacher Mrs. Marilyn Bartel who was also director of the Exceptional Chorus. This is where Adam soared to his highest academic and social achievements, which I will highlight later in his story.

After high school graduation, Goodwill helped Adam land a job on two occasions. Then, came that bump in the road when Adam went into, for lack of a better word, a funk. His EQ took a nose-dive but something he finally climbed out of over a period of several years. It has taken Adam ten years to dig himself out of that dark place he was in. At first, all the attempts to bring about a swift recovery from his depression were futile. Our last resort was psychiatry, which failed miserably because the mediations (without any real talks) turned Adam into a zombie. Thankfully, a kind Mr. Rogers-type clinical psychologist has proven to be the part of the remedy. I will revisit this time period later on in this memoir.

Paragon Adult Services also stepped into that void and offered Adam a safe home away from home. I write "stepped into" because the medications Adam was prescribed made him listless and unmotivational. As I indicated before, psychiatry with its tendency for prescribing pills was not the answer. But Paragon, which Adam attended on four weekdays was the other half of the solution and just the right prescription for Adam's residual Obsessive Compulsive Disorder (OCD) problem. Especially instrumental in that recovery was one of the staff members who encouraged Adam to be more outgoing. Adam still has some eating issues which, on the surface, do not interfere with his livelihood. They are only being addressed in order to make him less apprehensive. As a result, he is making use of these two services to this day.

We are elated that we have our "old Adam" back. His sense of humor has returned and he is able to enjoy his music. It's reassuring to hear the laughter coming from his room while he watches his favorite TV programs on his own TV. He has gone back to singing along with all the CDs he has. There are even times when we will catch him dancing to some of his favorite tunes. He has been motivated to the point where he takes our dog, Babie, for her "constitutional" walk three times a day. He sets and clears the dinner table each night and takes the garbage to the bins outside. The lessons learned here are patience and that even baby steps will continually go forward.

Our lives have been richly rewarded by the childhood innocence and yet words of wisdom coming out of Adam's mouth. Our cautious confidence resulted in all the smiles, laughter, and high jinks he showered upon us throughout these 43 years. Barb and I finally realized why the rear view mirror is smaller and the windshield is so much bigger: where you are headed is more important than what you left behind. We all need to be reminded that we don't always control circumstances, but we can control our response to those situations. We also sensed that, paradoxically, failing to make a choice is a choice.

Since my retirement from teaching in 2000, it's gratifying to see how my life has brought me to this enlightened point in time. I started to understand how much of Barb's and our lives have been affected by raising Adam. I have discovered that the further I get on in my life the more I am drawn back to Adam's birth. I want to see how my values were formed in those past 43 years. I now understand those things I didn't when I was younger; how those events have shaped my life so significantly. This is not just wistful nostalgia but opportunities for introspection which I want to share with everyone who reads this book.

At the writing of this book, our daughter Angela and her husband have bought a house with us, which is large enough to provide both our families with privacy and. yet, help us with those physical chores which we no longer are able to do. There are five bedrooms and four bathrooms spread throughout this one-story ranch style house. This beautiful new home will also provide Adam with a place to live until he meets with us again at a later date. Now we can sit back and enjoy!

9. New home with our daughter's family.
Adam's room is left of the front door

As a fringe benefit to all the readers, this book should give everyone a glimpse into a brighter outlook using humor as the "best medicine" throughout the journey of life with a Down syndrome citizen. Ralph Nader said it best when he reminded us that "in humor there is truth"

LIFE WITH ADAM

VIGNETTE 1

LOVE-INS ♣

As a child, Adam was a pure joy to have around. His googling and little vocalized "raspberries", accompanied by that inimitable smile, helped us forget all the cares we had about him. When he was an infant he would be lying on his "blankie" on the living room floor on many evenings. It was then that I would get down on my knees and baby talk to him. His eyes would tell me he knew what was going on. As I increased the volume of my voice slowly, he would start flailing his arms. Then, as my voice reached a crescendo, his eyes would grow larger and his arms would reach higher, and then Adam would let go of the loudest sound of glee. This little game would, which occurred on almost a nightly basis brought Adam and me such joy. Barb used to complain that she didn't know if that was good for his heart. Because he never turned blue or started to cry, I felt in my heart that it was doing him some good.

Because Barbara had him to herself the entire day, I would make sure that I got my time in also. Every morning at the breakfast table, Adam and I had what I called "love-ins". I would set him on the table facing me seated and give him a whole lot of honey-bunches of hugs. This ritual continued until he was too big to sit at the table and when he would sleep later on the days I went to work. \

Our kids, Jeff and Angela, enjoyed interacting with Adam just about as much as Barb and I did. Because they played with him, he was able to increase his gross motor skills and learn how to interact with others. In addition, to our benefit, we had two built-in babysitters. Now that he was almost two years old, we felt better leaving him alone with them. On one of those evenings, when we were out, his brother and sister decided it was time for him to walk. They were quite creative in the way they approached this challenge. They saw how Adam could stand while he was holding onto something, but would freeze and drop to the floor whenever he would let go. They decided to trick him a little. They gave him a nerf football to hold after he was standing, and then coaxed him to come to his sister's open arms while brother Jeff let him. The ruse worked! Adam was tricked into thinking that he was secure holding onto something. When we got home, Adam did the same feat for us. We were so proud of our kids who helped their little brother reach another milestone in his development.

*10. Learning how to take his first steps
while holding onto a football*

VIGNETTE 2

POSTER CHILD ✖

When Adam was three, his physical therapist nurse from Children's hospital told us that there was nothing more for her to do because he had achieved her goals for him. She suggested that he continue his early intervention plan by attending Easter Seal classes. They would be able to help Adam with vocal, social, and fine motor skills. These were daily morning classes which had only a handful of students. At first, Barb was not allowed to stay with him in the room but could observe his interactions through a two-way mirror.

11. Some of Adam's photo ops as poster child for Easter Seals

Easter Seals wanted to test Adam's speech after Barb told them he knew about 45 words. His teachers apologetically told her that Adam had said very little to them. Barb wanted to prove them wrong and asked if she could finally stay in the room with Adam. When he saw his mom enter the room, to the surprise of his teachers, he had all kinds of things to tell Barb in 45 words or less.

Now that Adam was no longer speechless because he felt he had something to say, the speech therapist was able to test him. After the testing, the therapist concluded that Adam would not require therapy. His tongue was not that enlarged that it would impede his speech. Barb was so happy that she drove home quickly to tell me in a hurried and excited voice that Adam did not have a "peach imspediment". We still laugh to this day at her tongue twister moment.

Because Adam's social skills grew by leaps and bounds at Easter Seals and because he was so affable, the Easter Seal Committee decided to make him1981's Easter Seals Poster Child along with another older boy who was physically handicapped. This meant special TV appearances, TV and radio ads, and other events to raise money for Easter Seals. We were so delighted with him when he appeared on Channel 12's Howard and Rosemary Show and when we saw the TV ads asking for donations to Easter Seals.

The media was kind to Adam and he responded in kind. At a bowling tournament to raise more money, Adam was there as a spectator. He was intrigued by all the hustle and bustle and loud noises in that huge colorfully lit bowling alleys. When a TV reporter saw the awe in Adam's face, he asked him what he thought. Adam quipped, "Just like thunder!". On the evening news that night, a pleasantly surprised anchor loved Adam's observation so much that he repeated his response, "just like thunder!".

There were so many other appearances which put our three-year-old in the spotlight that we were starting to get tired of all of the attention. It got so out of control that I had been called into the principal's office for taking off too many days. He advised me gently to limit my attendance at those events. I respected his admonition because he was a supporter of Special Olympics and proud that Marshall had many special ed classes in its curriculum. I heeded his advice and limited my involvement to the weekends.

Because Marshall High School had those special education classes, the students there were very supportive of and kind toward their fellow students. When my students found out about Adam and his connection to Easter Seals through the school newspaper, they wanted to help out. They received permission to hold a charity skate-a-thon in a church hall in Milwaukee on one Saturday afternoon. The money raised from admissions was donated to Easter Seals. To my gratitude, many of my own students were involved in this effort. I especially appreciated the kindness they showed to Barb and me.

Our lives returned to normal after a full year of "gigs" with Easter Seals. It was a learning experience for Adam and aided him in future exposures to the limelight and the stage. But, now we had to find a good pre-school for our four-year-old.

As parents we need to be advocates for our children, particularly when it comes to education. Adam's preschool special education class at Grant School was extremely helpful for Adam's learning growth. His teacher was especially wonderful with the kids. As Adam reached elementary school age, it was up to us to find a school, which would benefit Adam the most. I visited several schools that had special education classes where I observed many different teaching styles.

Barbara and I had set up a meeting with someone from the Central Office at Washington High School in Milwaukee. The special education administrator we met was unaware that I had already visited the school. He didn't know that I had already visited the school he recommended which Adam should attend. The school was in our district, but was not one I felt was suitable for our son's needs. Any time I see a newspaper on a teacher's desk, I am suspicious of how much time would be given to the students. The baffled and flummoxed administrator justified his decision this way: "If you are driving to Cleveland, you can get there just as well in a Ford as in a Cadillac." I immediately retorted, "Yes, but the Ford will break down more often." At that point, he handed me the pen and told me to fill in the bottom line with the name of the school Adam was going to attend.

VIGNETTE 3

"PEACH INSPEDIMENT" ✿

We learned early on that Adam's fissured tongue, a common anomaly in Downs kids, would not impede his speech and, consequently, Adam did not need speech therapy. In spite of that, though, Adam encountered the same difficulties the average child encounters while learning the English language. It doesn't come as a surprise that his first problem was with his last name. It continuously amazes me that Americans can easily use that four letter word starting with an "s", but have a problem with "Schissler". And, I regularly took offence whenever someone called me "Shyssler". As a German teacher I certainly was very familiar with what that pejorative sounded like, and meant.

12. Adam sporting his "Where's the Beef? Pin

Adam came up with his own original pronunciation. In his younger years, whenever asked what his name was, he would respond with "Adam Kelleesir">

Kelleesir's two-year stint at Grant preschool ended with a trip to Disneyland during the month of August. By this time he was able to communicate at a five-year-old level. Because he had been watching more TV those summer months, he liked to imitate the ads that appeared with annoying frequency during the shows. Our Kelleesir found one particular commercial quite entertaining. It was a hamburger commercial, where an elderly lady, in a bossy manner, would complain, "Where's the beef"? Well, Adam was so enamored with that old lady that he immediately picked up on that complaint and repeated it whenever it struck his fancy.

On that trip to Disneyland, with Adam's brother and sister and their two female friends, we stopped at many fast food places where our Kelleesir frequently wanted a cheeseburger (to this day still his favorite) with "flench flies" and a dash of "Where's the boef?" Because Jeff's girlfriend was getting fed up with Adam repeating it all the time even in the back seat of the station wagon, she purchased a pin with that slogan on it to keep him quiet. To our surprise Adam was satisfied with that arrangement. Another of his favorite dishes at the family restaurants was that all-too-often mispronounced "pasghetti".

Although Adam was not on our two trips to New York, he didn't mind staying with his aunt while we were in "You-Nork, You-Nork". What his problem with the name of that city was, I can't say. I must confess, though, I used to have a hard time saying Massachusetts, Oconomowoc, and Kinnikinic. To my amazement, Adam had no trouble with those names.

On another visit out West in Aunt Kathy and Uncle Rollie's van, the radio was playing the country western song, "River Road" by Crystal Gayle. We all burst out laughing when Kelleesir sang along with "Wiveh Woad". I still have no idea why he had problems with those R's. He did eventually correct all of those "peach inspediments" and speaks well enough to be understood for the past few decades.

It is worthy to note, though, that the young Kelleesir wasn't the only one who had difficulties with some of the words in English. His sister would always suggest something with the phrase, "I have an eye-dye"`. We would answer with "What is your idea?" My mother, whose first language was not English, would come up with some doozies of her own. She would call irrational people "hidiots" and talk about "bequipment" and "containyers". Her funniest malapropism was when she introduced to us a new kind of cone-shaped munchy Bugles as "Buggles". In all honesty, it really is those little quirks or idiosyncrasies which add humor and great memories to our lives.

VIGNETTE 4

JOURNEY

We loved to travel every summer as a family. We had made four trips out West before Adam was born. Two of them were road trips all the way out to California. The first vacation was with our elderly neighbors who gave us the travel bug, and we've been out on the road again for over two dozen times, interspersed with trips to Europe during Easter vacations. Adam was only 15 months old when we took him all the way to the top of Pike's Peak in Colorado. When my mother found out, she scolded me sharply saying "What's the matter with you, taking that child all the way up to the top of the mountain with his bad heart". My only rebuttal was, "Ma, he didn't have to climb it and, besides, he was breathing better than I was."

From all those experiences I came to realize how travel is educational in so many ways. It occurred to me that the more mobility a person has, the less that individual is educationally strapped. This is the reason for less restriction of access to buildings and other places like parks and outdoor environs for physically handicapped individuals. That easier access to more places invigorates and expands their minds as well as ours.

Barb and I always wanted to travel to see all those beautiful God-made creations, which this country has to offer. We preferred the western half because of its variety of topography with all the vistas and places which fulfilled our adventurous spirit. We continuously took Kelleesir along with us because we knew he would hardly complain about anything. He particularly enjoyed the restaurants and the motel pools. He was peculiarly fond of Best Western motels and would call out from the backseat, "Look there's the crown, the crown! Let's stay there", whenever he saw the logo.

In addition to the education and enjoyment travel affords, there is another fringe benefit attributed to it. Travel guru Rick Steves has alluded to this in many of his travel guides and TV specials, but I feel that Mark Twain said it best when he wrote, "Travel is fatal to prejudice, bigotry, and narrow-mindedness, and many of our people need it sorely on these accounts. Broad, charitable views of men and things cannot be acquired by vegetating in one little corner of the earth."* I've maintained that if anyone is uncomfortable around people and things that seem "foreign" to them should stay at home with a National Geographic Magazine. But, that also has its limitations because staying at home and reading a book has even been panned by St. Augustine who wrote, "The world is a book, and those who do not travel read only one page." *

13. Checking out the Best Western pool in Salida, Colorado

After Adam's godparents moved to Raleigh, North Carolina, we were given another reason to travel, this time to visit our cousins. These trips afforded scenic rides through the Smoky Mountains and two visits to Dollywood. Adam's fondness for country western music was augmented by those strolls through a really less crowded theme park at that time.

Every spring and summer break provided opportunities for family outings to many locations in Wisconsin like Wisconsin Dells, Door County, Little America, and Green Bay. The boat-trip on the Wisconsin River was always a relaxing ride while surrounded by the natural beauty of the dells. Door County offered some New England vistas and different kinds of cuisine highlighted by their famous fish boils. Little America had rides which weren't as wild and had much shorter queues. This less crowded ride park was also less expensive than Great America or Disneyworld. Even though Green Bay had different venues that tourists would visit, the "Frozen Tundra" at Lambeau Field and the home of Adam's favorite team, The Green Bay Packers was the main attraction. To Adam's delight, on a few of those trips, my mother and father would come along. Grandpa would sometimes tease and grandma would scold, but Adam loved the attention which his grandparents showered on him. Now that Barb and I are grandparents also, we have discovered that our responsibility was to spoil our grandchildren. Adam was regularly assured souvenirs ala grandma and grandpa on all those excursions.

But the most memorable outings in Wisconsin were the two and three day stays in my brother and sister-in-law's lake house in the Chain-of-Lakes area in Wisconsin. Cousin Jada would accompany us on those trips up North. My brother owned a large pontoon boat which made the "little vacation" more adventurous. It was Adam's first time fishing and he was delighted with the wiggly little life forms hanging from the end of the line. He was delighted every time the red bobble bounced around on top of the water. On those warm days we would dock the pontoon near a sand bar and enjoy the warmth of the water by sitting in fold up chairs in the shallow ends. On each of those outings, my brother "Uncle Buncle Irv" would let Adam navigate the pontoon through the larger bodies of water, and even an occasional channel. He would be beaming with such pride!

The evenings would end with a car trip to the ice cream parlor in a small fishing town at one of those Chain-of-Lakes. Ice cream is Adam's favorite dessert. Any flavor is satisfactory, but "navilla" with chocolate syrup is still his favorite. Even though the Chain-of-Lakes are at least a three-hour-ride, we never heard him plea, "are we there yet?" Being with family was always a complete and satisfying vacation for Adam.

However, not every place was enjoyable for our Kelleesir. On one of our road trips out West, we had forgotten how literal Adam took words at times. We thought that we should do something we'd never done before and go visit a ghost town. We were already in California and, at the last minute decided to see Calico Ghost Town. The billboard indicated that it was a mere 12 miles away.

As it turned out, the place was right in the middle of the Mojave desert, which gave the town an even more deserted look. The plaque at the entrance indicated that Calico used to be a 19th century mining town.

Parking the station wagon turned out to be much easier than getting Adam out of the car. While we were all out of the vehicle, he was holding on to the steering wheel so tightly that I had to pry his hands carefully off of it. Then, I had to just about carry him into the town to make any progress. All that time he held tightly onto my hand as we made the walk around the sandy streets of that peopleless town. Strangely, we never saw any other tourists around. I thought to myself: this is really a deserted desert town.

Talk about being clueless. Not even Jeff or Angela understood what was happening at Calico. It wasn't until weeks later, when we were watching our slides, that it dawned upon us that Adam didn't understand what a ghost town really was. Adam, of course, was afraid of encountering real ghosts. I'd be afraid too! Sadly, because of our ignorance, it traumatized him for Disneyland, which was only a couple of hours drive away and was certainly not deserted.

The cobblestone streets surrounded by colorful and inviting buildings brought a bright smile to our six-year-old. Mickey and Minnie welcomed Adam. Even Pinocchio sat down with us for breakfast at one of the many restaurants in Disneyland. He was captivated by the animatronic dancing bears in Frontierland and enjoyed the Small World water ride immensely. It was quite captivating for me too. ♪ "It's a small world after all" is still an "Ohrwurm" for me to this day.

14. Donald Duck scared Adam with his
well-known "peach inspediment"

Everything was just wonderful in Wonderland until we entered the famous Haunted Mansion. Again, our propensity for not understanding Adam's literal mind eluded us. He refused to walk into the mansion. Barb had to pick him up and carry him into the building and into the elevator waiting for us passengers. Barb informed me that Adam was literally clawing his way over her shoulder, terrified. Unfortunately, it was too late to turn back. As soon as we sat inside the little tram which would take us around in the ride, I put Adam in my lap, and to protect him from his fear, covered his eyes with my hand during the entire ride. Looking back now, we feel awful that we put Adam through that harrowing experience. When we went to DisneyWorld in Florida the following year, we avoided the Haunted Mansion at all costs. There were no deserts or ghost towns in Florida either.

***15. Some scary characters trying to escape
the Haunted Mansion thumb-how***

The one thing I do recall about that trip to Florida was that we were so excited to go the next morning, we were unable to sleep. Barb and I decided to get out of bed and leave right after midnight. We didn't have to wake Adam because he was not sleeping either. The car had already been packed the evening before and so we went out to the garage, left a note for Jeff and Angela on the kitchen table, and headed out in our brand new vehicle. We advised Adam to go to sleep in the back seat, but I noticed that he wouldn't sleep. Whenever I looked into the rearview mirror, I saw little racoon-like eyes looking back at me.

That trip to Florida was filled with other kinds of unique experiences. It was the first time ever that Adam's glasses fogged up as soon as we got out of the car at a rest stop. Five minutes back onto the road, it started to monsoon to the point where I had to pull off to the side of the highway. And, then just as fast as those cloud bursts arrived, they departed and the sun returned to steam the road we were on. I came to eventually realize that we had made the mistake of going to Florida in August. The heat was oppressive during the few days we spent in the Orlando area and Disney World. Adam never complained.

Because his godparents had relocated to Raleigh because of my cousin's job transfer there, we would spend some of our Easter vacations with them in their spacious home. Adam enjoyed those stays and loved seeing his "first love" Krissy, who had continually doted over Adam when he was just a toddler. The cookouts, trips to Myrtle Beach, and the battleship moored on Cape Fear brought smiles of enjoyment to the three of us. Angela and Jeff were old enough to stay home and enjoy their spring break without parents around.

VIGNETTE 5

HOLY EMANATIONS! ✖

16. Brother Jeff donning his altar boy
apparel at Christmas Eve Mass

Comedian Steven Wright once said, "Going to church does not make you a Christian any more than standing in a garage makes you a mechanic" * Adam's love for his fellow man, his great regard and respect for family, and his constant politeness makes him a model Christian. He follows the precept that the 10 Commandments are not multiple choice. He is a spiritual person and hasn't had to prove it by going to church every Sunday. However, that didn't mean that he didn't attend church along with the rest of us.

Yet, he was sometimes confused by the entire process of attending the Mass. Adam's first misconception about church was that it was somewhat contractual. Whenever that basket was passed around, he thought that it was the admission charge for the mass. I don't know whether he was that far off. Many of us ask things from God by promising to do this or that in exchange, The basket aside, his favorite part of the mass was the singing, which he made sure everyone around him heard. His least favorite part of the mass was the homily which is supposed to be, according to Webster's Collegiate Dictionary, "a usually short sermon". To my mother's displeasure he would fall asleep and lean against my father's side who would be sitting in the same pew with us. My father would laugh and gently nudge him awake. Adam was under that impression that when we sing, we pray twice and, so, he had already done his part,

They say that "out of the mouth of babes come words of wisdom" Adam might have been about seven years old at the time, the age of reason, when he made his beliefs known to the entire congregation. The priest had just made a point during a rather lengthy homily, when Adam blurted out loudly, "Yah, right!" This commentary produced muffled giggles from some of the surrounding pews. Dad and I were laughing, while my mother was mortified. Barb wasn't too happy either because she thought that we shouldn't have encouraged him that way. Barb was even more upset with my dad and me whenever we snickered at Adam's conclusion to the Hail Marys with "and blessed is the Fruit of the Loom, Jesus."

There was another time that Adam broke the silence at another mass at another church. This time it was at a solemn funeral mass for his great aunt. We were sitting in the front pew, with emphasis on "Pew", when Adam let one fly. It was tremendously embarrassing to us because the volume of the spent gas echoed throughout the entire church. This was one of the few times that Barb and I were disappointed by his lack of manners. I didn't laugh this time.

VIGNETTE 6

TV OR NOT TV? ♣

Contrary to what many experts think about what's bad for kids, most of the TV programs and movies Adam watched had a positive effect on his learning and behavior. Sesame Street played a major role in this pre-school education. But, not all TV or movies were good for Adam's consumption. One of his favorite movies was "Clue". The board game for him was too complicated but the silly comedy in the movie was something he could relate to. This was during the VHS era. An annoying thing about the tapes is that Adam could rewind and play forward, rewind and play forward, rewind and play forward, rewind and play forward. Maybe, it's because repetition is the mother of all learning.

Adam was in his pre-teen years when I received a call from a 9-1-1 operator while I was in my basement office working on my computer. I knew that Adam was upstairs watching something on the TV. The operator was quite concerned because she said that someone from our house had called to report a murder. Because this was the time Adam was binge watching "Clue", I immediately knew who made that call. After I explained that the call had actually come from a son with an overactive imagination, I was admonished severely by an angry person on the other end of the line, and that the next time a fine would be assessed.

Adam's imagination played another trick on us, which brought concern to an entire school system. It was at the very beginning of his sophomore year that I received a disturbing call from the school psychologist at Hamilton High School. Apparently Adam had told a teacher that he was going to commit suicide. This, of course, raised all kinds of red flags for the school. At this stage in his life, Adam had never shown any type of behavior or said anything remotely assigned to thoughts of suicide. He was a thoroughly happy kid enjoying his classes and interaction with his fellow students.

Out of surprise and less of concern, I immediately spoke to the psychologist at my school. Dr. Bob and I had become good friends over the years when we both worked at Marshall High School. He was just as surprised as I was because we had spoken frequently about how well Adam had adjusted to all of the schools he had attended. Since Bob knew the psychologist at Hamilton, he did a little digging into the report. Of course, Barb and I also looked into the matter. Well, to make a long story short (Adam here would say at this point, "too late"), after questioning Adam where he would have picked up on such a disturbing idea, and which contradicted everything we knew about him, he responded, "I heard it on 'One Life To Live'". We were so relieved to find out, "I want to kill myself" was nothing more than the influence of the melodrama unfolding on many a soap opera.

As parents we all know about the bad influence of some television programs, many times forgetting its powerful influence. Today parents have even more concern about the dangers presented by cell phones and computers. This Adam incident, however, preceded the cell phone and computer era. One evening, while we were watching the film "Mississippi Burning" we had forgotten that Adam was in the kitchen nearby and heard all the N-words which were used profusely at the beginning of the film. As soon as we sensed that he was in all likelihood listening, we told him to go up to his room to do his homework.

The next day we received a phone call from the vice-principal. Our presence was requested. He explained that he needed to meet with us about Adam's use of the N-word in one of his classes. When we met, we told the vice-principal that, if it was anyone's fault, it was ours because of our lapse in judgement the night before. We explained that Adam did not really know what the word meant because we ourselves never used it. And that word was so out of his character. It was, though, an opportunity for a teaching moment. After we explained to him how hurtful that word was, we never heard Adam use it again. He continued to prove it by the TV shows and movies he preferred for his entertainment.

So many of the sitcoms that Adam enjoyed watching on his TV in the privacy of his bedroom were what he called "wholesome". He would giggle at "Welcome Home, Kotter", belly laugh at "I Love Lucy", and laugh with "Laverne and Shirley". The closest he has come to a suggestive show is the old sitcom "Three's Company" and that's mild compared to what TV has to offer today.

One of the more relevant TV programs and one Adam easily identified with was the series "Life Goes On" (1989-1993) which showed what family life was like with a Down syndrome son and brother. That role was played by Chris Burke, an actor who actually had Down syndrome. According to one of the reviews, "During the show's first year, the main focus was on Charles "Corky" Thatcher. Much of the show examined the challenges of a family whose son had Down Syndrome. The Thatchers sought to have Corky interact with regular society after spending years socializing him amongst other kids with Down syndrome in 'special classes'. The need to integrate Corky into normal society was Season 1's main storyline, as the Thatchers opted to enroll Corky in a regular high school despite the principal's demand that he be placed in an alternative program for those with Down syndrome."[*]

The fact that Corky had two siblings made the TV series also more relevant and popular with brother Jeff and sister Angela. Without a doubt, it did wonders for Adam's self-worth watching someone like him act in a major TV drama. This was just a prelude to what Adam himself was going to accomplish in the ensuing years. But for now, Sunday nights would be spent on the living room couch watching the story unfold.

His love of country western music, which he also calls "wholesome" prompted him to watch "Hee-Haw" on Saturday nights. Every year he looks forward to watching the Country Music Awards (CMA). His favorite artists are the hall of famers like George Jones, Garth Brooks, Johnny Cash, and Vince Gill.

I still don't understand the attraction that Pro-Wrestling has on Adam and so many of his friends. It does appear to be quite violent, yet I know he realizes that it is fake like the Wile-E-Coyote and Road Runner cartoons. I guess he enjoys the bluster and chest pounding which is par for the course with all of the pro-wrestlers. In his youthful years, he was deathly afraid of and, therefore, disliked the "Undertaker", but admired the tough-talking "Stone Cold Steve Austen".

A real sport that Adam is fanatical about is football. It is no surprise either that he is an avid follower of the Green Bay Packers. He lives and dies with each of their performances. Whenever they lose, and thankfully that doesn't happen too often, he sulks the entire rest of the day. It takes him longer to fall asleep after the night games. I'm glad that with my experience coaching high school boys and girls, I am able to help him overcome his disappointments. Typical of armchair quarterbacks, he mostly blames the refereeing and coaching. In spite of his scowling, I enjoy watching the Packer games with him anyway.

Today Adam's room is a veritable man cave decorated with all kinds of Packer memorabilia. His prized possession is a signed 24 x 36 inch poster of Bret Favre. But it's not only Packer "stuff" hanging on the walls. Plaques which he won for bowling and track and field decorate his room. There are also trophies on his shelves for the various sports he participated in at Special Olympics events. He has a shadow box full of medals and ribbons, which are symbolic tokens of his feelings of self-esteem.

As a coach, I have always maintained that there are lessons students learn out on the field or any indoor sports venue, which they will not get in a classroom. They will find out how they perform under pressure, both physically and mentally. They learn teamwork, but understand their own individual responsibilities. They will learn how to take loses and not blame the referees. They are taught how to be gracious in victory--valuable lessons they can use going forward in their lives. However, I never failed to emphasize that they were students first and athletes second, and that I was a teacher first and a coach second. As with Adam, I reminded them that they should not judge their self-worth by their lack of success in any athletic endeavor. They should not define themselves that narrowly. This is probably the hardest thing to swallow because there are coaches and parents who will be too judgemental when it comes to their young athletes' performances.

VIGNETTE 7

IN SICKNESS AND IN HEALTH�֍

As I've pointed out before, our first 10 years with Adam were what we want to call our "Amoxicillin era". Adam's lungs were still not mature enough to fight off the viruses, which came uninvited into our household every winter. Our little guy's first hospital visit was when he was a tender two-year-old. What started with just a deep cough developed into a full-blown case of croup. At the time we failed to realize that the airways of Down syndrome children are smaller and that the windpipe is narrower. We were told that croup is a parainfluenza which irritated Adam's upper airways causing them to swell and, therefore, impeded his breathing.

I wasn't home the evening that Barb called the doctor, worried about the bark-like sound of Adam's coughing and, now, his labored breathing. The doctor had recommended that she turn on the shower and stand there holding Adam with the curtain drawn to allow the steam to help him with his cough and breathing. Even though she immediately followed the doctor's advice, it worked only temporarily, because Adam started to turn blue in his face, Barb then called the fire department immediately. The fire truck and paramedics arrived in five minutes accompanied by an ambulance ready to take Adam to the hospital.

Before Barbara hopped into the ambulance, she called me from home to let me know to meet her at Children's Hospital downtown. It was getting late into the evening, when the hospital physician informed us that Adam did, in fact, have the croup. I became extremely concerned when I asked the physician if his condition could result in death. She nodded to the affirmative. Out of grave concern now, we never left Adams' side while he slept inside the oxygen tent that night at the hospital. The morning brought sunshine and Adam sitting up in his bed, smiling and tapping at the sides of his transparent tent. He probably felt that this was a much neater tent than the one we created at home with his afghan. The nurses told us that they loved his infectious smile which found its way through the clear plastic during Adam's waking hours.

Adam slept better than we did those two critical nights inside his tent. With every little noisy breath we looked up to make sure he was alright. As the morning approached, his breathing was less shallow and sounded more normal. According to the nurses, Adam's fever broke and he was well on his way to recovery. We surmised that because he was beginning to enjoy the hospital food! That was the best sign. He left after three days for home with sighs of relief from a pair of happy and relieved parents. Jeff and Angela greeted him with smiles and open arms.

*17. On one of those sleepless nights with an
ailing Adam with his pet bunny*

The following year brought another visit to the hospital. This time it had nothing to do with a virus, but more with a vehicle, in this case a Tonka dump truck. He was bent over holding onto the back of the truck when the wagon part flipped up and hit him on the forehead. The sharp metal edge on the truck immediately produced a cut on his forehead about four inches long and deep enough to require stitches. Thankfully, Adam did not look into the mirror attached to the front closet door where the mishap occurred. We didn't panic either because we did not want him to "freak out". We told him we were going to go to see the "nice doctors" at the hospital. Adam remained calm in the car while Barb held a clean towel to his forehead.

Emergency checked us in immediately and we went to a small room in the ER area. Adam's toddler-size body fit nicely on the table where the nurse cleaned off the area around the cut and gave him a local anesthetic. Adam's entire face and neck now were under a white sheet that had a small rectangular opening over the injured area.on his head. The entire time the doctor was stitching the wound, Adam was talking away under that sheet, which would heave up and down with every word spoken. Now he had all of us in stitches. Barb and I attributed the babbling to possibly a case of nerves.

At least Adam didn't drink Lavoris like his sister Angela or eat the mushrooms growing out on our front lawn. With the Lavoris incident I tried to make her vomit by putting my finger down her throat. She bit me and I almost had to go to the hospital for stitches. Instead Barb called the poison control department at Children's Hospital where the doctors recommended that she drink some warm milk. That did the trick after a quick trip to the bathroom toilet.. As for the mushrooms, we had to go to the Emergency at St. Joseph's Hospital to have her stomach pumped.

We delayed Adam's next trip to the hospital for a year. He was going into his tenth year with his annual ear infection followed by an amoxicillin cocktail. This time we were aware of Adam's physical makeup when it came to his inner-ear. His cochlear tubes weren't slanted downward enough and, as a result, any fluids from his head colds would collect in those narrow passageways and cause the infection. We went to an eye, ear, and nose specialist (a colleague of mine called them sarcastically "eye, ear, nose and pocket book specialists), who recommended he put tubes in his ears to remedy this annual problem. We talked it over and decided not to put Adam through all that discomfort and see what the winter would bring. If the earaches continued then we would go ahead with that procedure. Luckily, since that time, Adam has not had a single ear infection. We chalked the cure up to his face and head going through adolescent maturity. However, his narrow windpipe created an even more dangerous incident.

"John, get your ass up here! now!", screamed my wife Barb from the kitchen upstairs. By the time I ran up from the basement stairs, she had already dislodged the piece of beef that was caught in Adam's throat. Thank God that as a nurses' aide she had learned the Heimlich maneuver for she had just saved Adam's life. She was still shaking a half hour later from that harrowing experience. Adam, fortunately, was no worse for the wear.

Adam's heart, ears, and lungs matured nicely, but by the time he was six he needed glasses. I'm not sure whether he ever needed them at that time. The optometrist assured us that Adam, indeed, was in need of them. Now, as we look back, I'm not sure whether Adam understood the doctor's directions or just aimed to please. We know from years of experience that Adam would tell us what we wanted to hear and not what we actually wanted to know. We learned to ask questions that were not as direct or suggestive. Instead of saying, "Does your tummy hurt?" We would ask what's wrong and where does it hurt?" Instead of asking "did you spill the milk", he would blame that elusive child in our household named Idunno". We're glad that we listened to the optometrist because he still needs glasses to this day. In all honesty, sometimes the simplest solutions were a bit more complicated with our little Kelleesir.

On a more positive note, with the exception of his last hospital visit when he was 31, Adam has been healthier than the rest of his immediate family. (Yet, I will need to visit his mental life altering syndrome later on in this narrative.)

As an adult now in his early forties, he has never had a cavity. That's because he doesn't eat candy or sweets. But, he will enjoy a piece of birthday cake whenever that situation presents itself. He doesn't eat between meals except for his bowl of ice-cream at exactly 8:30 every evening. I will explain that also later. He isn't obese and has a great blood pressure. He has low cholesterol and sleeps well every night. I told him that after he lost his 20 pounds, I found them on me. Since he is so healthy, he is no longer afraid of his yearly doctor visits.

Now that Adam's older, he gets grumpy at times like all of us folks. However, we never heard him complain about having a headache or muscle aches or even belly aches, even though Downs people age earlier. He enjoys a healthy lifestyle due to his mother's home cooking and making sure that he is not a couch potato. The house we live in now is much larger than the former, and even trips to the kitchen or the attached garage from his room yields a little exercise. Since both Barbara and I are getting more forgetful in our older age, Adam has done a lot of the footwork for us and has turned into a wonderful gofer.

VIGNETTE 8

OOPS! ✖

Adam was a well-behaved kid and never gave us reason to reprimand him, but to only correct him in certain situations. And, once in a while his curiosity would get the best of him. On one of those incidents of curiosity, I was baffled by the number of negatives that were left on the film in my camera. I didn't recall taking as many photos as indicated on my new camera. I questioned Jeff and Angela. They both blamed Idunno. After I finished the roll a few weeks later, I took it to Walgreens to have the film processed. When I went to pick up my photos I looked at them right away, curious to see what photos I had actually taken. There's the cliche that a picture is worth a thousand words, Well, in this case, nine of those photos spoke volumes. Each one of those nine "selfies" revealed the culprit as Adam, a.k.a. Kelleesir. Curiosity had gotten the best of him.

***18. Caught red-handed using Dad's camera
while inventing the first "selfie"***

To say that life with Adam was sometimes unconventional is an understatement. He had some peculiar habits which frequently tested his sibling's patience and understanding. After he graduated from the crib to a single bed in his brother's room, he would alarm Jeff and us by breaking the night's silence with a loud thump. Falling out of his bed had become a common occurrence until we fitted it with a portable bar that we slipped under his mattress.

Then, poor brother Jeff had to endure nightly hummings while Adam was chewing and gnawing on his thumb, sitting up and leaning against the wall by his bed. Jeff would have to wake Adam and remind him to lay back down. Adam did this with such frequency that we saw the effect of the thumb-chewing on his calloused, larger right thumb.

Adam has had constant issues with volume and portions. Whenever he poured his own milk, it had to be all the way to the brim of the glass. He soon discovered that trying to take a drink then was a lot more challenging. We didn't cry over the spilled milk, but he continued to do the same thing with other beverages, which we eventually had to correct by watching him pour the drinks.

When soap became available in pump bottles, Adam would use half of the bottle to wash his hands. As far as his Windex fetish, he would use more of it to clean his glasses than the family in the film "My Big Fat Greek Wedding". Everyone but Adam has learned that you can't put toothpaste back into the tube. We still have to put the toothpaste on his toothbrush for him or he will go through half a tube in a couple of days. In his defense, though, he never got any cavities.

I recently noticed that Adam was going through pencils at an unusual rate. I soon discovered that, in spite of the pencil sharpener on his desk, he thought that as soon as the pencil was down to its wood, it was no longer usable. However, to his credit, he didn't chew the eraser off his pencils like his older brother Jeff used to when he was younger. Maybe it's because Adam doesn't keep his pencils long enough. I never chewed on my erasers either. One of my grade school nuns, who aren't supposed to lie, told the entire class that one of the ingredients in the erasers was cow dung. Holy Cow!

When he was older, we were afraid to hand Adam any shaving cream in an aerosol canister. We had visions of Adam having a shaving cream fight unwittingly with himself. As a result, we purchased an electric razor for our young man. Even that device had challenges for him. To this day, he insists on shaving anywhere else except in front of a mirror. Maybe the past photo op encounter with the mirror over the fireplace mantle still made him dislike how it reflected on him. Years of experience has enabled me to master the art of shaving without a mirror, but Adam has to shave for at least 15 minutes in each session - not so much that he has a thicker beard, but that he has a difficult time with the correct angle for all three rotary blades to do their job all at once. He also had to learn to be more careful minus the mirror because he shaved off one of his eyebrows a couple of times when he was still learning to locate his entire beard.

Then, there is Adam's moniker given to him by his uncle Rollie. Because of his infatuation with the sounds of flatulence like the one a whoopee cushion makes, he is now dubbed "Adam Fladdam". Ii might be a dubious honor but, nonetheless, a nickname he lives up to just about every day. To further his fame for flatus, his mother dubbed his duds "thunder wear".

And, it certainly didn't help that Dr. Oz validated farting by telling every one on one of his shows that smelling farts was good for us. * He even brought along a large capped jar of them for people in the audience to test (for what I don't know). I wonder whether Dr. Oz meant smelling ours or others'? I am still inclined to believe that it was healthier for Adam than for the rest of the family.

Adam was in good "gas company", though, when he joined the Exceptional Chorus at Hamilton. I guess there were other fans of flatulence who had to be reminded by their teacher to "Mind your manners!", an admonishment followed by a chorus of giggles and a few red faces.

Adam's loss of manners would always be a source of his own laughter. Adam's sudden giggling was frequently a giveaway as to his unexplained laughter. Yet, he will also giggle if he hears anyone say "gas, blast, wind, rip, or blow" in any context whatsoever. I am still reminded about the scene in the film "Rain Man" when the main character Raymond played by Dustin Hoffman is in the phone booth on the road to Las Vegas with Tom Cruise, who plays his younger brother. Without warning, Hoffman announces "Oh, Oh, fart", which immediately emits a response from Cruise about the terrible odor. Hoffman actually did "break wind" inside that narrow telephone booth during the filming of that scene. To this day, Hoffman claims that, surprisingly, it is his all-time favorite scene. So, admittedly Adam is in good company.

Adam didn't miss the opportunity to embarrass me in unfamiliar surroundings either. It was on the way back from one of our road trips to visit cousins in Raleigh, North Carolina. I think we were in Kentucky and had to stop at a fast food restaurant to pick up something to drink. Adam needed to go to the men's room and I decided to accompany him. No sooner did we open the door to the bathroom, when a man standing in front of the urinal, with reckless abandon let go of a sonic boom. Adam immediately yelled, "Yukkkk, he farted!" Before the "gentleman" turned to address Adam's shock, I yanked him quickly into one of the stalls, put my hand over his mouth because he was just about to let go with some uncontrollable laughter. His body was shaking from the muted laughter, and I had to fight from laughing myself. Too embarrassed to face the farter, we waited for the man to leave the restroom before coming out of the stall to relieve ourselves.

For some reason Adam will surreptitiously or willfully save up all of his gas until we are in a vehicle with closed windows. He was already a young adult when he went along with his Uncle and Aunt and us for a destination wedding in Colorado. The reception was held in the ski village of Breckenridge. The altitude of this ski area made it difficult to move around too quickly and we had to pace ourselves. We envied Adam because the altitude didn't seem to bother him at all. Of course, he was younger and leaner. However, it just might have been the altitude, which had that one negative effect on him prompting my brother to give him the title "Adam bomb". It was colder at those higher altitudes and so we had to keep the vehicle's windows closed. It was then that we had to beg him to "mind his manners" those cold mornings in the van that we had rented for our extended vacation in Colorado. I have only gone to great lengths to point all of this out to show this loss of manners on Adam's part is not exceptional.

And, just as a footnote of sorts, I was recently informed by Adam that there was a World Wrestling Federation (WWF) professional wrestler in the early 90's, Bryan Clark, named "Adam Bomb" at the time. I am certain, however, that he was known more for ripping his colorful shirt. Sorry, I couldn't resist.

VIGNETTE 9

EXCEPTIONAL GROUP ♣

German philosopher Friedrich Nietsche once wrote, "Without music life would be a mistake"*. And Adam's life was not a mistake when he showed his love for music early on in his "career" as singer and dancer with An Exceptional Chorus, a career which has now spanned over 27 years of his life. We always knew the importance of music in early education. How do we think we learned the ABC's? Didn't "Sesame Street" use music as its main medium of information. It's no wonder that "Sesame Street" along with "Mr. Roger's Neighborhood", was Adam's favorite show as a toddler and into early childhood. He watched both every day and learned so much from these TV classics, while being musically entertained.

Music has consistently played a major form of entertainment in the Schissler household. Jeff used to sit on his rocking horse and rock to the music I played on the Hi-Fi stereo. He sang in the church choir and now, already in his fifties, he plays the bass guitar and sings in a local band. Sister Angela learned guitar and was a member of the Angelaires at her high school. She and her friends have also sung in church at weddings and other functions. My father used to play the accordion and guitar at wedding receptions when he was younger. With me, that musical talent must have skipped a generation, although I did promote music as often as possible. So, it's no wonder that Adam also benefited from and became part of a musical family.

It's too bad that music and the arts are not considered as an integral part of a person's education. What happened to teaching "the whole child"? Too many times, it is seen as entertainment and, hence, something that is not as important as the academic classes. I find that somewhat hypocritical because sports, more of a form of entertainment, is an integral part of high schools' curricula. Even in higher education, like college football, for example, it's a religion.

19. Adam's early, insatiable need to plink around on a piano

I am reminded of an anecdote which proves my point about the importance of music. During the holiday season there were all types of professional people invited to a cocktail party at a prominent person's cocktail party. With cocktails in hand, the guests made their rounds talking to the other invitees. One of the conversations which was overheard was between an older man and a younger woman. The gentleman introduced himself to the lady by proudly stating, "Hello, I'm Doctor Smith. I am a thoracic surgeon and I save peoples' lives. What do you do?", looking down at the shorter individual standing in front of him. She then quipped, "I'm a musician, and I make those lives endurable".

Without a doubt, when Adam joined An Exceptional Chorus more than 27 years ago, this wonderful school based organization was "just what the doctor ordered" for our budding social butterfly. While attending Hamilton High School in Milwaukee, the chorus opened another whole new world to him. The encouragement and guidance he got from the chorus director, Marilyn Bartel, was transformative. This chorus had its beginnings more than 30 years ago as a special education class. To point out what can be accomplished by these special people, the following script showcases those successes:

"'An Exceptional Chorus' Inc. from Milwaukee, Wisconsin is a chorus of cognitively disabled, physically challenged and autistic young men and women. All these young men and women have a dream -- a dream to show people what their abilities are, not their disabilities.

"This dream continues to grow as these young people perform for a variety of organizations, ranging from senior citizen groups, professional men and women's organizations, to formal dinner presentations. The group performs during the day and also evenings and weekends, if requested....

"The group also offers a Christmas Show during the Holiday Season. Past shows have included a Bi-Centennial History, a 50's Danceland, a Country-Western show, a Star-Spangled Patriotic show, a sweet glimpse into the past with an 1890's to 1920's revue, a Millennium Show and a Tribute to the USO.

"...The chorus has performed throughout Wisconsin, traveled and performed at the Capitol Building and Lincoln Memorial in Washington D.C., successfully auditioned and performed at Disney World in Florida three times...They have performed at the Grand Opera House in Dubuque, Iowa, at the Mall of America to a standing ovation of 1000 at the National Down Syndrome Convention in Minneapolis, and in 2005 performed in Toronto... while doing collaboration with the Famous People Players...These students are TRULY EXCEPTIONAL!*

20. The cover from one of the benefit booklets featuring the chorus

When An Exceptional Chorus was in full swing, our up-and-coming entertainer looked forward to the weekly Tuesday evening practices at Hamilton High School. Adam began his stint with the chorus in 1993. This chorus is proof of Milwaukee Public Schools' constant innovations with curricula. An Exceptional Chorus is only one great example of how we can encourage students who already have coordination problems to dance, not just individually, but as a group.

Within those 27 years in the Chorus, Adam grew many friendships. His pleasant disposition made him popular with his fellow singers. The chorus teacher, Mrs. Bartel, took his raw talent and honed it into a fine musical skill. Adam also had help from Mom, who spent many nights with him practicing the lyrics and the inflections required for the honest rendition her soprano needed to hear and see.

21. Adam wearing a satisfied smile after
one of the Christmas concerts

VIGNETTE 10

EXCEPTIONAL TOURS ✿

*22. The Chorus made the TV news for one of
their recent benefit Xmas concerts.**

[Note the misspelling of "sparkle". When Barb and I asked Adam to spell it, he did it correctly without forewarning. Even the pros could use some help from these "exceptional" people.]

Adam and the Exceptional Chorus' past performances included several appearances at Disney World, The Grand Opera House in Dubuque, Iowa; Milwaukee Brewers Baseball game; Milwaukee Bucks basketball game; Mall of America, National Down Syndrome Convention in Minneapolis; Tripoli Circus and an appearance at the Welk Resort Theater in Branson, MO.

The group's talents made news everywhere and, as a result, this exceptional chorus had over 100 gigs in the Milwaukee area and in the neighboring states. Adam took part in the majority of those sing-outs in the past 27 years with this Hamilton High School based chorus.

23. Adam singing "Achy-Breaky Heart"
at one of his many performances

Because of the early intervention strategies and excellent education provided by the Milwaukee Public School System, Adam was able to develop valuable social skills, which made him more likeable and outgoing. With that type of encouragement from home and school, Adam was able to grow his self-image and gave him the confidence to do many solos at the many Exceptional Chorus events. These were song and dance routines delighted all the audiences in the many venues the chorus was invited to. Adam sang Billy Ray Cyrus' "Achy-Breaky Heart", while the entire chorus line-danced to it. He did a great rendition of "I'm a Yankee Doodle Dandy" while dancing with a cane and tipping his hat to the audience. He was even Frank Sinatra in a hat and overcoat singing "New York, New York". He finally overcame "You Nork, You Nork".

*24. Adam as Tevia singing and dancing
to "If I Were a Rich Man (1997)*

However he is still best known for his role as Tevia in "Fiddler On the Roof". I am still amazed, as was the audience, at Adam's ability to remember the monologue, which preceded the song, and the dance he did to the lyrics of the song, "If I Were a Rich Man". In his vest, old captain's hat, and baggy pants, he would belt out the lyrics almost as well as anyone else on Broadway. His teacher eventually revealed to us that Adam would always be her Tevia.

Another benefit Adam received while a member of An Exceptional Chorus was his exposure to R&B music, tunes from Musicals, Rock 'N Roll, Jazz, Blues, and many other musical genres. Now our Tevia has added to his repertoire an eclectic collection of CDs.

Adam's participation with An Exceptional Chorus, also offered him many opportunities for travel and, thereby, more help with his social skills. His musical skills were already being honed, as well as his dancing abilities on the stage. In contrast to the car rides to the events in the Milwaukee area, some of the trips now involved rides on a tour bus to the various venues in the various states. Some of those trips required overnight stays at motels as well. Social interaction was part of the entire experience and proved to be helpful. Happily, These situations presented fewer problems for Adam because he had already experienced these with us just about every summer.

Those trips which were too long for a tour bus afforded Adam his first airplane ride. To familiarize him for his first flight, we took him to Milwaukee's Mitchell Airport, where the friendly folks introduced him to their occupations by allowing him to walk through one of the empty planes and to sit in the captain's chair. The actual plane ride was going to be headed for Disney World in Florida. That trip by air was followed by two more invitations to Orlando to perform at Disney World. Those years in the early 1990s were wonderful for our growing teenager!

Barb and I have never been to Washington D. C., but our Adam went there "on tour", and performed on the steps of the

Lincoln Memorial. The chorus was invited there to sing the patriotic songs they had practiced for this special occasion at a special location.

Of course, those trips were the only time Barb and I experienced the empty nest syndrome. Barb missed him especially. She felt that the house was too quiet without him. To compensate for that feeling of solitude, we decided to get some respite care of our own at various vacation spots during those eight days without Adam.

VIGNETTE 11

GIRLS, GIRLS, GIRLS ♪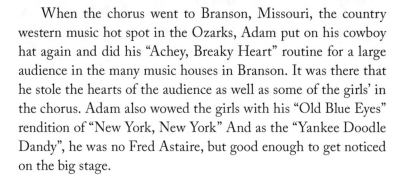

When the chorus went to Branson, Missouri, the country western music hot spot in the Ozarks, Adam put on his cowboy hat again and did his "Achey, Breaky Heart" routine for a large audience in the many music houses in Branson. It was there that he stole the hearts of the audience as well as some of the girls' in the chorus. Adam also wowed the girls with his "Old Blue Eyes" rendition of "New York, New York" And as the "Yankee Doodle Dandy", he was no Fred Astaire, but good enough to get noticed on the big stage.

25. The "Wholesome Kid" from Milwaukee, Wisconsin

During those 27 years with the Chorus, Adam didn't find it difficult to make friends and, as he got older, he became more interested in girls. The girls already had their eyes on Adam. It was inevitable that he would return their winks and smiles. His first girlfriend was his Dolly in "Hello Dolly". She was a delightfully talented girl who became his co-star in other roles in their many famous musical performances, during their "going steady" period.

They went together for many years, including to Homecoming Dances, proms and other school related social events. They, of course, saw each other every Tuesday night at practice as well. The young lady came to our home often and we had numerous gatherings at restaurants with her parents. One could say that they were quite the item. Some of the chorus girls were even envious of the puppy love they were witness to.

As the years passed, Adam's girlfriend would also attend our family events. One of those gatherings was at his cousin's wedding reception in Waukesha, about 25 miles from our home. They

danced, ate, and drank non-alcoholic beverages the evening long.
They had a good time, but it was getting late as Barb suggested we
leave for the long ride back to Milwaukee. My wife and I climbed
into the front of the car and the happy couple slid into the backseat.

Because it was dark and because I frequently get lost in
Waukesha, I missed the expressway entrance and wound up on
one of those unlit, narrow country roads. In the dark, I heard
some rustling in the backseat and asked what was the matter.
The young lady responded matter of factly, "Mr. Schissler, Adam
won't kiss me!" I nearly drove the car into the ditch and, then, had
to muffle my snickers as Barb came to my rescue by explaining<
"Well, maybe Adam is just too tired." I thought to myself, "What
happened to that innocence?"

Now this wasn't the first time Adam was "hit on" by a date in
the backseat of a car. B. D. (before Dolly) There was a Homecoming
Dance, to which Adam had invited this tiny, cute teenage girl. She
was delighted and so were her parents when Adam presented her
with a bouquet of flowers. We took some photos and then went
to the car. This time Barb and I were on a well-lit expressway. So
I could see through the rear view mirror, his date pawing away at
Adam while rhetorically asking and almost purring, "Are you my
big tiger?" This question was proposed several times, probably
because Adam did not respond right away. On the way back, after
the dance, the mood was more subdued though.

Adam did give his "Dolly" a going steady ring at the last
Christmas they were together. Alas, they broke up a few weeks
later because she felt Adam was not paying enough attention to
her. In all honesty, she was correct. Adam never liked talking on
the phone and never bothered to call. I don't think he understood
that a ring meant more of a commitment; something, we guess,
he wasn't ready for.

He gave dating a third try with a girl he met at his adult
center. He was trying to get her to enjoy the center's activities and
succeeded somewhat, but he was flummoxed by her unwillingness

to participate in the activities which would have helped her come out of her depression. He knew from personal experience what she was going through. He had her over at our house several times and took her on some outings. The staff at the adult center praised Adam for his efforts to bring the young lady out of her introverted personality. He was especially disappointed that all of the evening phone conversations with her did not produce better results. He learned the hard way that the road to hell is sometimes paved with good intentions. After a few months, She never showed up again to the adult center. Adam gave up trying and felt that it was her loss. It was at that juncture that he wasn't going to deal with women anymore because they were all "too high maintenance."

Alas, as is the case with many human experiences unrequited love is one of the most painful. While Adam was at his adult day program at Paragon he was particularly smitten with one of the staff who was 15 years younger. To his great disappointment, she told him that she was going back to school to get her degree. With rue his heart was laden! At that point he told me he was finally done with women and wanted nothing more than enjoying life as a middle-aged adult at his home with the two people he loved the most,

So, at the age of 43, extremely content with living with us, and not at present able to make any new friendships because of the Covid virus, we don't know whether Adam will ever marry. Some of his friends did marry and some got divorced. He understood the reason for us staying home was to stay safe, but that didn't make him feel better, except for the realization that we were protecting him from catching the virus.

Before Adam was a client at Paragon Adult Services, he was gainfully employed at several businesses. In spite of the fact that Adam cherished country western music because it was so wholesome, there was one unwholesome line from a song that created a problem between him and his employer. Adam had been working at a McDonald's for only a few weeks when he was fired by the manager. This was his first job and he wanted to impress his boss by taking off the paper wrapping tips on all of the straws at one of the tables. When the manager got on his case about it, he told her "Take This Job and Shove It". In his defense, however, he explained to us that he didn't like being made fun of by some of the other employees at this location.

People can really be cruel at times. His second job was with a large chain grocery store as a packer. He had been working there for a couple of years and things were going well for him at the registers. Because the store was nearby, I would pick him up after his day shifts. On one of those days, I had just walked into the place while he was still at the register line when I heard a disgruntled customer tell the cashier, "I don't want him packing my groceries". The cashier turned red and didn't say anything, but appreciated me budding in by telling her I was there to pick up Adam. He punched out and, after we were in the car, I told him that some people were not as polite as he was. Adam responded confidently, "That's OK. I was Employee of the Month twice already".

When we got home, I told Barb what had occurred at the store. She then told me about an incident a few months before when she was standing in line with Adam and a cart full of groceries. She turned around after she heard some laughter and saw two adolescents pointing at Adam and making funny faces. Barb immediately exclaimed, "What are you looking at that's so funny?" They immediately became quiet and stepped out of the line. Barb went on to tell me and our Emloyee of the Month, "I sometimes expect that kind of behavior from dumb teenagers, but not from a older woman who should know better. Shame on her!"

To the credit of humankind, Adam did not encounter too many people who were that insensitive. Many of the workers and bosses were kind and not patronizing in any obvious ways. We found most of them to be helpful and understanding.

VIGNETTE 12

ALL IN THE FAMILY ♣

74

*26. Adam's family: Mom, Dad, brother,
sister, in-laws, niece and nephews.*

The actor Michael J. Fox described to a tee how Adam feels about the most important people in his life. Fox said, "Family isn't an important thing; it's everything". *

I've already explained how Adam enjoys watching the older family sitcoms. It then makes sense to invoke Michael J. Fox because he was one of the main characters in the sitcom "Family Ties", This was one of the TV shows Adam would binge watch after recording them on his DVR. It was among some of his favorite family shows. Adam has alway felt extraordinary ties to his family. The sentiment expressed by Michael J. Fox perfectly describes the shared DNA he has with our families. That DNA flows persistently through Adam's veins.

My roots and Barb's go all the way back to Europe. My great grandparents, grandparents, parents, and I were born in a small town in the Slavonia area of Croatia. Barb's grandparents and father were also born in that Slavonia area not far from my birthplace.

In 2015, to celebrate our 50 years of marriage. Barb and I decided to actually reconnect with our own family ties Our daughter Angela and granddaughter Jada came along with us. Barb and I traveled to my homestead in that small hamlet where I was born. When we arrived we were treated like royalty by all of our distant cousins. They made us feel more like close family members than strangers. I discovered the important role family plays in the Croatian culture, but I never imagined how strong those familial feelings made up their mores. Our hosts in my hometown of Velika Pisanica couldn't have been more kind and considerate.

Not only did I reconnect with my relatives but Barb, with my relatives' help. was able to find her father's birthplace. It was then that we discovered that her father was born only 20 miles from my birthplace.

All the meals we shared with those families in those three memorable days have become the fondest of memories. These tasty meals were more for conversation than for just consumption.

Each dinner involved stories about relatives and relations. They proved that family was the foundation of their society. To this day all the travel guide gurus will tell you that the best way to start any conversation with Croatians is to inquire about their families.

27. Three generations of Schisslers in front of my ancestral home in Croatia

It was about a year after we had traveled to Velika Pisanica that one of our hosts shared a post on Facebook about a philosophy professor who summed up the importance of *familija* with an interesting metaphor. The following is the translation of the Croatian version (author unknown*):

"The professor stood before his class and had some items in front of him. As soon as the class started, without saying a word, he raised a large empty glass jar and started filling it with golf balls. He then asked the students if the jar was full. They agreed that it was.

"The professor then took a box of small stones and poured them into the jar. He shook the jar lightly. The small stones rolled and filled the open spaces between the golf balls. He asked the students again whether the jar was full. They agreed that it was.

"Then he took a box of sand and poured its contents into the glass container. Of course, the sand filled in everything else. He asked once more if the jar was full. The students responded with a unanimous yes.

"The professor then pulled two bottles of beer from under a table and poured the contents into the glass jar, effectively filling the remaining spaces in the sand. The students started to laugh.

"When the laughter subsided, the professor said, 'Now I want you to recognize that this glass jar represents your life. The golf balls are important things--your family, your children, your health, your friends, and your favorite passions--even if everything else was lost and only they remained, your life will always be filled. The stones are the other things like your job, your house, and your car. The sand is everything else--the small things.

'If at first, you put the sand into the jar,' he continued. 'there won't be any room for the rocks or golf balls. The same goes for life. If you spend all your time and energy on small stuff, you will never have time for the things that are important.

'Pay attention to the things that are important for your happiness. Spend time with your kids. Spend time with your parents. Visit your grandparents. Go there with a second dinner. There will always be time to clean the house and mow the lawn.

'Take care of the golf balls in the jar, and put them in first place. Set your priorities. The rest are just sand and stones

"One of the students raised her hand and asked what the beer represented. The professor smiled and said, 'I'm glad you asked. Beer only shows that no matter how full your life may seem, there's always room for a few beers.' The nods and instant laughter from the students in the lecture hall proved to the professor that his points were well taken."*

At the writing of this book, the Covid Virus had been raging uncontrollably in Wisconsin, and even more so in the Milwaukee area. The virus had made all of us reevaluate our priorities when it came to family. Because the virus' source was so contagious and dangerous, Adam was saddened by the lack of contact with the relatives he was used to having around. In addition to missing his relatives, he also missed his friends at chorus and his adult activities program at Paragon.

The chorus practices had been modified. Even though there were outdoor practices at someone's large yard and social distancing was observed, Barb and I opted to keep Adam at home. We also did not want him to go to the daily adult program at Paragon on the south side of Milwaukee. This. of course, presented much dismay for Adam who, just like the rest of us, wanted to mingle with his friends. However, he has his niece, nephew, sister and brother-in-law as his four main friends in our household. Whenever he expressed frustration, I reminded him that when it comes to friends it is better to have four quarters than 100 pennies.

Thankfully, since we've moved, Adam now has a large, bright room with a built-in desk and bookcases. There are four ceiling to floor windows facing the front yard allowing him to observe all the joggers and dog walkers on the campus directly across the street. He now enjoys walking our dog Babie two or three days in our expansive front yard. Babie's breed is "teddy bear" which makes her more of a lap dog than a guard dog because it wouldn't take a burglar too long to notice her in the dark because she is all white.

Adam also helps with setting the dinner table for us seven diners. The meal is then accompanied with stories of the day's events and other conversations. According to Adam, the family that eats together stays together. This is so important that he will get upset if someone doesn't come to the table.

Of course, in spite of our frequent family dinners in the dining room, Adam still misses his friends and the ability to socialize with them. To his credit, though, he does not comfort himself with food. Unlike us, he doesn't eat between meals. This takes a lot of self-control for all of us because Barb is an excellent cook. Nonetheless, all the meals she makes are wholesome and always include vegetables, frequently tasty salads. Adam loves vegetables and salads, but looks forward to the main courses. Nothin' says lovin' like somethin' from Mom's oven.

Adam's only vice is that nightly dish of ice cream that he has at exactly 8:30. (Remember "Wapner at four"?) His favorite flavor is anything that looks like ice cream. He religiously carries the bowl at 8:35 with that creamy treat ala smile to his bedroom like a priest carrying a chalice of communion wine. You can set your clock by it. For some reason, this ritual brings a lot of satisfaction to our Rain Man.

VIGNETTE 13

―――

OLDIES BUT GOODIES ✿

28. In the car with Elvis, Buddy Holly and "Johnny B. Goode"♪

As I've stated before, when the Covid virus hit the city in 2020, life with family took on even greater importance in Adam's world. He missed the gatherings with his aunts, uncles, and cousins.

But with the introduction of Skype, Zoom, and other amazing technological achievements, he is still able to connect with our families and talk to them via a LED screen.

With the absence of chorus practices, Adam has turned his attention to the love songs from the 50's and 60's for his musical needs. To humor him I call them "oldies but moldies", which I play on the Sirius XM station in the car. He looks forward to the errands I run while sitting next to me in our new sedan.. Like my son, I enjoy those classic sounds as well as his company.

When I ask my adult son what it is he enjoys about this genre of music, he sticks true to his standard, which is the "wholesomeness" of the lyrics. There are no F-bombs or angry words or yelling with these oldies. The slower songs, which were called "ballads' in my day, all deal with love or tell a story. What better thing to sing about than "amore"? The fast songs are more upbeat and there are actual attempts at harmony. He especially enjoys the tunes where the singers' voices are used in place of musical instruments. But those 50's tunes with the silly lyrics are his favorite… "da do ron ron ron, da do ron ron." Here is a list from his personal hit parade:

♪ "The One-Horned, One-Eyed, Flying Purple People Eater"
"Christmas, Christmas Time Is Here"
by Alvin and the Chipmunks
"Does Your Chewing Gum Lose Its Flavor
on the Bedpost Overnight?"
"Baby Talk" and "Baby Sittin' Boogie"
"Itsy Bitsy, Teeny Weenie, Yellow-Polka Bikini"♪

In addition to the nostalgic elements found in music, Adam and I enjoy looking at the family pictures, slides, and videos. Photography is a hobby of mine, a hobby which has produced over 3,000 slides, and more than 50 photo albums which are presently stored in a special room in our basement. I have about the same amount of video cassettes of many of our numerous vacations, but most are of family gatherings. One could say I have a plethora of pictures. Adam loves to look at these, and the many family videos I have taken over the past 27 years. He is, of course, especially fond of the older ones.

Another one of Adam's wonderful personal attributes is his sense for humor. Nobody loves a good laugh more than he does, and I am always there to accommodate him. Probably, because I taught three different languages, I have a propensity towards word play. What better word play is there than the pun? I will sometimes tell him, "Well, and well is a deep subject", then apologize and follow up with, "Sorry, didn't mean to **pun**ish you", and if that wasn't punishment enough, I would finish with, "Sorry, but that was only 2/3rds of a pun, P-U".

Another form of word play is what I call ricochet words, where the second part of the phrase bounces back to the first part. These repetitive sounds make him giggle with their rhyme. Some of Adam's favorites are, of course, "Adam Fladam", then "burpus on purpose, "itsy bitsy", and" brain drain", just to cite a few examples. Finally Adam will get belly laughs from my questions like…

"Why do we park on driveways and drive on parkways?"
"How can you cut a tree down and then cut it up?"
"Why do ships carry cargoes and trucks carry shipments?"
"I don't waste my food, because my food goes to my waist."

I can't take credit for coming up with all of these because, as comedian Steven Wright said while slowly pacing the stage in a pensive manner, "To steal ideas from one person is plagiarism. To steal from many is research."* Ralph Nader and many others have said that "in humor, there is truth" *. And, in truth, I must admit that I have borrowed a few for this book. With apologies to Steven Wright, here are some beauties Adam and I have pondered and which made us laugh and nod our heads in acknowledgement:

"The early bird might get the worm, but the second mouse gets the cheese".

"Never take a sleeping pill and a laxative on the same night".

"A bank is a place that will lend you money, if you can prove you don't need it"

"I don't want a doctor who just practices medicine.

"Why is abbreviated such a long word?"

"When you choke a Smurf, what color does he turn?"

"Change is inevitable...except from vending machines

"How do you tell when you're out of invisible ink?"

"I need to have an open mind but my brains keep falling out." *

All those kinds of witticisms like the ones listed above continue to entertain Adam and me immensely. I believe that humor reflects the human condition, which everyone can relate to and, hence, is so popular. Occasionally though, the humor is lost to some because not everyone is privy to the same human condition. A case in point: when "Rain Man" came out, Barb and I traveled miles to the movie theater to see it immediately. It was worth the ride and effort.

We found the film most entertaining and true to life, especially true to our lives. However, some of the audience didn't find the humor in a number of the events because Barb and I were the ones laughing out loud during the entire viewing. Those giving us looks of displeasure didn't realize that we were living with our own Rain Man.

Even though Adam is not a savant in math like the main character in the film, he has other special skills, which I will address later. Nonetheless, he does, to this day exhibit some of those same idiosyncrasies as Rain Man, most of which can be so endearing.

We didn't take Adam along with us to the cinema that evening because we weren't sure how he would react or understand at that young age. Later on, he watched it with us when it finally hit the

TV airways. He enjoyed watching it. He understood that there is nothing wrong with laughing at our own unique foibles.

The other day, while we were stopped at a red light, the car in front of us had a bumper sticker which read, "Hug your kids at home and belt them in the car". That immediately brought a smile to his face and a short chuckle. I love those moments with Adam when we can laugh at the world and share some of those common sentiments. And to use a car metaphor, he has come to the realization that the longest word in the English language is "smiles" because there is a "mile" between both of those *s*'s.

VIGNETTE 14

RED-LETTER DAYS ♣

29. *"It's not what's under the Christmas tree that matters, it's who's around it".* Charlie Brown.*

The Christmas season is, as it is mine, Adam's favorite time of year. Adam brings the kid out in me every yuletide season. His favorite decoration is the Christmas tree and Barb and I make sure that it meets with Adam's standards. all the different types and sizes of artificial trees we've had over the years have always met his approval. That Tannenbaum was always the centerpiece of our living room. The Christmas village with lights and the electric streetcar became another important piece of our yuletide tradition. The Christmas creche with all the figurines will be found in a prominent place in the living room.

Admittedly, I am one of those people who pushes the Christmas season. If it were up to Adam and me, Christmas would start right after Halloween. For us, Christmas is not about the gifts, but more about all the colorful decorations which brighten up our homes, inside and out. Although, lately I have given up climbing on ladders to decorate the house with lights, there is still a great amount of effort and love put into the placement of shining decorations.

The other wonderful Christmas traditions are the songs and carols, particularly the older ones which enhance those feelings of nostalgia during this particular holy season. Thanks to the chorus, Adam has learned and sung many of those classic carols. He loves singing along to them whenever they are playing on the car radio. He also listens to and dances to the Christmas CDs in his room.

Naturally, we have a large collection of those CDs, yet Adam's favorite CD is a time-honored Reader's Digest collection of Christmas songs. One of his favorites songs is "Winter Wonderland", whose lyrics I had altered a bit to get a laugh out of Adam. We sing these with impish enthusiasm. The newly adapted lyrics are:

♪ "Later on we'll perspire
As we sweat by the fire
The pants that we've made
Walking in our winter underwear" ♪

Our other son Jeff was never told that these are not the original lyrics to the song, and was scolded by his music teacher at his Catholic grade school for singing that altered version. When asked where he came up with those lyrics, he told on me! I'm glad the good nun didn't call me in for a conference for contributing to the "delinguacy" of a minor.

The day after Thanksgiving is our green Friday, not named for money, but for setting up and decorating our Christmas evergreen. The Reader's Digest CD will always be playing. And, just about the time Pavorotti sings "Ave Maria", tears well up in Adam's eyes. I, then, also get teary-eyed as a mixture of emotions begin to well up in me also; the beauty of the song's melody combined with the eloquence of the Latin language. That aria brings back those memories of my days as an altar boy when the true meaning of Christmas was stronger than it is today. When I asked Adam why he was crying to "Ave Maria", he explained that it reminded him of his grandma, Maria Schissler. He explained that he remembered that it was played at her funeral. My mother was very special to him and he felt the loss deeply, as well as the loss of his grandfather who was no longer there to tease him those five years earlier.

"It's a Wonderful Life" is his all-time favorite Christmas movie. He has a VCR tape and a DVD of this classic. He has played it so many times that he is able to lip sync Jimmy Stewart's every line. He knows all the words by heart. He can also give the word by word rendition of Scrooge's dialogues and monologues for three of the "A Christmas Carol" renderings. But with the Muppets version of this classic, he just sits back and enjoys a bit of tiny timfoolery.

Even though National Lampoon "Christmas Vacation" is somewhat naughty, Adam gets the biggest bang out of the squirrel, cat, and sewer gas incidents. That particular film is one that I will sit through and watch with him just for fun. I enjoy the feast for your eyes color and the newer Christmas songs this film offers.

Every year, though, I sound like a broken record around this time when I ask Adam why Santa Claus has problems with gifts at Christmastime. "If he knows when you are sleeping and he knows when you're awake, and he knows if you've been bad or good...why in the heck doesn't he know what you want for Christmas?"

A man after my own heart, Adam will play Christmas songs in his room even during the summer months at times. Adam takes Christmas in July literally. To be sure, Barb and I have never encouraged this practice; but it does serve another purpose. In the fall, An Exceptional Chorus already starts in September with Christmas songs in preparation for the Holiday Benefit Concert in December.

Since celebrating Christ's birthday is important to Adam, it should come as no surprise that he considers family birthdays also a reason for celebration. Since siblings, parents, in-laws, nephews, and nieces are all part of his entire family, birthday parties have become frequent events. These celebrations always involve a birthday cake, replete with candles, balloons, ice cream and singing. He loves watching and enthusiastically clapping his hands for the celebrants opening their gifts after blowing out the candles on the cake.

Summer offers Adam many more outlets for entertainment. The family barbecues are at the top of his list. Again, it's not so much about the food, but more about the people. He laughs every time I call his Mom "Barbi-que". He frequently joins us on the patio when we have all the outdoor mood lights hanging on the eaves to provide heart-warming ambience. Life is good!

Another one of Adam's happy holidays is Halloween. I have a theory that it is because it's so close to Thanksgiving. And that means there will be more family gatherings and festivities, closely followed by the Christmas season. Even though Adam is not into candy, he finds it fun to hand it out to the trick or treaters, The fact that he can dress up as anyone he wants appeals to him as well. He has won first prize for his Superman costume at one of the chorus'

Halloween parties. He has also gone as the Undertaker of WWE fame, and as Dracula. One of Barb's favorites was when he went last year as a box of crayons.

30. "Mosaic" Adam ~Life is like a box of Crayons

When he is not busy partying, Adam likes playing board games like Clue, Monopoly and Sorry. His favorite card games are War, Go Fish, and Old Maid. Since he has always had a great sense for fairness, he will become quite annoyed if anyone cheats and will call them out on it. Adam's sense of fair play is one of his strong suits.

Whenever the weather is suitable in Wisconsin, Adam likes to take our pooch Babie for a walk. He now has a large front and back yard that allows Babie to search for some olfactory gold. She is his watch dog who sleeps in his bedroom every night and will wake us if she hears any strange "beeps" from the detection devices connected to our ceilings. However, she would not be a good guard dog because her breed is "teddy bear" and she loves everyone and would probably lick the intruder to death. For Babie's convenience there is in front of our house a fire hydrant, which Babie can sniff and discover who the latest visitors were.

VIGNETTE 15

AVANT SAVANT♣

Adam is certainly no Einstein but, with that aside, he has shown signs of surprising intellect and intuitiveness. Barb and I attribute this to the help and education he got from the community organizations and the public schools he attended and is still participating in. Friends and family have told us that we also had something to do with his intellectual and social skills, because we had realistic goals for Adam so that he could be the best he could be.

Divine intervention could also have played a role in Adam's wonderful achievements. A very dear colleague and mentor, Elaine Steiger, was so supportive during those difficult months and even years after Adam's birth. She buoyed our emotional toughness with her strong sense of faith. Of all the saints, every Catholic knows what kind of great intellect St. Thomas Aquinas was. To this day, I don't know how Elaine acquired a relic (a piece of bone) of the saint. It was presented to me safely secured in a beautiful reliquary and even came with a document of authenticity, signed by the Pope. It is presently in a safety deposit box in our bank.

However, the relic was not so much for us as it was for Adam. Elaine advised us to place the reliquary on Adam's forehead at bed each night, and say a prayer for God to keep our son safe, healthy, and successful in the challenges ahead. Yet, Barb and I have always believed that God also helps those who help themselves and we continued, with St. Thomas' aid, to help Adam help himself.

As the years went by, Adam certainly felt comfortable inside his own skin and didn't suffer from an identity crisis. For example, when he was still sharing a bedroom with his brother, I was in the small hallway nearby about ready to go down for breakfast when I peeked into the room to see Adam struggling with the belt on his morning coat. Totally exasperated, he threw the belt down and declared, "I'm such a retard!" When he saw me, he laughed and asked for help. As I wrapped the belt around his waist I assured him that he was not a retard and that his fingers were just not made for fine motor tasks like tying things. He still has difficulty with small buttons and anything that involves the pincer grip. Talk about having self-awareness, even though his comment was self-deprecating.

I recall another incident at our two-storied house on Girard Avenue. Jeff was coming down the open staircase and stopped half-way to show off his latest hairdo which had a predominant part in the middle. He didn't ask for my opinion but, in spite of that, I quickly quipped, "Well, guess every block has to have an alley"

To which Jeff replied, "Yah, well at least I don't have a parking lot"

And then Barb had to chime in, "No, just a parking lot with snow banks"

Adam loves that kind of repartee, and still laughs at moments, which allow us to laugh at ourselves.

I don't like climbing ladders anymore and therefore no longer put lights on the gutters or eaves. The placement of those Christmas lights used to be a yearly ritual. On one particular November day, our son Jeff was over to help with the hanging of a string of lights. I was on the ground carefully feeding Jeff the lines and holding the ladder. While the task was tedious, Jeff and I passed the time talking about past Christmas decorating. It was at this point that Adam surprised us with this very astute observation. "Ah, nice, father and son bonding".

By the time Jeff got married to his fiance Molly, Adam had already bonded with Jeff. It was the June of 1979 that Molly and Jeff were going to marry. Adam was excited because he was now going to see all his cousins again at the wedding reception. To prove his fondness for his brother and future wife, Adam surprised us when he asked us during the wedding dinner if he might make a toast for the couple sitting at the head table. He was an 11-year-old at the time and there were some people at our table who questioned whether Adam had the wherewithal to make that toast. My mother was especially chagrined by his request. But we knew otherwise and encouraged Adam to make his toast. Adam got up, faced the bride and groom, and while holding his goblet high, he announced loud enough for everyone to hear, "Jeff, I love you because you are my brother. Molly, I love you as a sister-in-law. Welcome to the family".

31. Adam toasting his brother and his sister-in-law Molly

Adam was just as proud of himself as we were of him. My mother's fears were assuaged when everyone else clapped and also raised their goblets high. That toast was one of the highlights of the evening.

At another evening dinner, when there was still a full nest, typical of a teenager who will put blame on parents, Adam made this observation: "First you had Jeff, and raised him as a boy. Then you had Angela, and raised her as a girl. Then you had me and raised me as retarded." Now this came out of nowhere and caught us totally off-guard. Angela and Jeff laughed, but I didn't know how to take him until I remembered a quote from Mark Twain: "When I was a boy of 14, my father was so ignorant I could hardly stand to have the old man around, but when I got to be 21, I was astonished at what the old man had learned in seven years".* A little smirk from Adam's face told me that he was just kidding and was happy with his station in life.

Here is where the real savant quality reveals itself in Adam and more proof of how important family is to him. He has this amazing ability to tell us the names, relationships, dates of birthdays, graduations, marriage, anniversaries for his siblings, nephews and niece, his uncles and aunts, and his numerous cousins. He is our savant when it comes to all of their ages also. He especially remembers the dates of his grandparents' and great-grandparents' passing. Whenever we or his relatives can't remember any of those dates, celebrations, or even names, the consensus always is "Let's ask Adam".

Another category Adam is particularly helpful with is when we forget the name of a movie, movie star, or TV show. There are frequent times when Barb and I will see a face and not remember the name of the celebrity on TV. We will call Adam out of his room and ask him to identify the star. Not only will he give the name, but he will let us know the title of the program or the movie that star was in.

On one of the days he was at the Paragon Adult Center, he surprised the staff and clients with his knowledge about the Green Bay Packers. Not only was he able to identify the players but, to the staff's amazement. he even could tell them the names of the head coaches and the years they coached going back all the way to Vince Lombardi. In typical fashion when someone challenged him about some Packer trivia, he was constantly ADAMant about the reliability of his information. Adam's favorite Packer is quarterback

Aaron Rodgers, even though he has a 24 x 36 autographed poster of former quarterback Brett Favre.

Adam continued to wow the folks at Paragon with his knowledge of the names of the people in the political arena as well. He was able to name all the US presidents and vice-presidents from 1968 on to the present. Along with the dates they served, he even was able to name their opponents. I still have a difficult time naming those opponents myself.

Some people are just good at names and some are not. As I've gotten older that skill has been diminished by age and possibly by my former occupation. I used to be good at names. As a teacher I had to be, but now I sometimes have a hard time with the names of people I should remember. I am of the opinion that because I had so many names to keep in mind as a teacher, that portion of my brain is now fried from overuse. In more likelihood, I believe my 77-year-old brain has something to do with it. I am grateful that there is an internet which helps me frequently with those names and pertinent information.

Adam's knack at mind games like "Trivia", "Catch Phrase", and "Brain Quest" are surprisingly extraordinary. He is so proud of himself when he is able to get more answers correct than his surprised opponents. He claps for himself and grins like a Cheshire Cat in *Alice In Wonderland*, like a *Wunderkind*.

Even though he hardly reads books, he gets his information from the things he reads and hears on television. However, as a former teacher of English, I know that writing is one of the most important critical thinking skills, more than even reading. To his credit Adam has already gone through dozens of notebooks where he writes down his thoughts about the things he has done in the day. He writes these journals on an almost daily basis. So, Adam does read and write. I am reminded by a quote from Pam Allyn, author of 27 books on education, "Reading and writing cannot be separated. Reading is breathing in, writing is breathing out."*

VIGNETTE 16

DEALING WITH LOSS ♣

The first 32 years of life with Adam were just fine except for those first ten winters with amoxicillin. The next 22 years were smooth sailing and we happily watched Adam succeed at school, in athletics, at work, and with the chorus. I've indicated before, the challenges of being a parent never end because life happens.

An endoscopy in 2011 precipitated Adam into a five-year period of melancholia and, as is always most often the case, there were extenuating circumstances, which I will disclose later. To understand Adam's condition these are the events which led up to his fears and melancholia:

- Sept. 2010. He burned four of his fingers pulling an apple pie out of the oven. The heating pad slipped which resulted in third degree burns to his right hand. This mishap prevented him from work for nearly a month. He never shed a tear.
- Oct. 2010. He learned that we had to put down our dog Dolly, who was his friend for 16 years and who stayed in his room with him nightly. He never shed a tear.

- Nov. 2010. He began to overeat at Thanksgiving and the holiday parties.
- Dec. 2010. He witnessed a friend from chorus have a gallbladder attack, fall on the steps of Hamilton when paramedics had to be called…no tears.
- Jan. 2021. Adam learned that his favorite Exceptional Chorus teacher was retiring from the chorus. He never shed a tear.

He never cried about any of these events, but must have internalized them since these didn't hit him right away. We only learned much later that this delayed response was common with Down syndrome adults.

Around New Year's Eve he started to complain about pains in his chest. Out of concern for his heart, we took him to a clinic to have him checked out. The doctor there diagnosed it as gastritis. We could have told Adam that it was just heartburn, but we knew how literally Adam took scary words. The doctor prescribed some acid reflux medication and sent us home. In spite of the medication and in our rush to judgement, we grew unsure about the reason for the discomfort, (he called them pokings") which he was still experiencing in his chest.

So, a few days later we took him to St. Luke's Hospital Emergency Room for more extensive tests. The doctor there also suspected gastritis and ordered an endoscopy for the next morning. That meant he would have to stay in the hospital overnight. My reaction by using the expletive, "Oh no" showed my worry, which Adam picked up on immediately. I had forgotten how children and even adults will react the way we react to a situation. Barb saw the concern in my eyes and the fear in Adam's eyes. She decided to stay the night with him in the hospital.

Even though the endoscopy went well and confirmed what the doctors had diagnosed initially, the word "heartburn" was branded into Adam's mind for the next five years. The fact that he heard on TV that former President Clinton had had a heart attack just added more fuel to his heartburn. Our efforts to rename Adam's condition as acid reflux failed miserably.

Adam was not reassured with the diagnosis because he claimed that the pains continued. Maybe they were psychosomatic or were just ghost pains? Because of the worry over the pokings in the center of his chest, Adam became slowly uncommunicative and lethargic. He would walk around in a daze which then turned into him moving mechanically like a drill team member. Paralized with fear, he stammered and talked slowly. It was like he lacked self-direction. His bed wetting, spitting at a mirror to see if he still had saliva were most worrisome. He lost over 20 pounds because he ate so little. We even went to the extreme of feeding him chocolate shakes on an almost daily basis to have him regain a healthy weight. In spite of our constant words of support and reassurances, Adam was just trading one emotionless and worrisome behavior for another.

It was time for professional intervention. We had hesitated to take our depressed son to a psychiatrist because we knew that our troubled son would just be prescribed some strong medications which had some serious side-effects. The psychiatrist we took him to didn't even ask Adam anything other than his name and was more concerned about Adam using a Kleenex to rub his nose while he kept logging "stuff" into his computer. He then prescribed citalopram. This made Adam even more lethargic and flat-lined him emotionally in just a matter of days. After three visits, we told the doctor, "don't call us, we'll call you".

We took the next step deciding to go with a psychologist, someone who would actually talk to Adam. Barb and I were frustrated with Adam not telling us what was bothering him so much. He would sit in the dark, was non receptive in positive situations, and I discovered too late or was too distracted that Downs people process negative information more slowly. I was not aware of this until I purchased the book *Mental Wellness in Adults with Down Syndrome:*

"People with Down syndrome often have a delayed grief response. For example, when a family member dies, the person with Down syndrome may initially seem to be unaffected. Typically, s/he will begin to grieve approximately six months later...Understanding that a loss has occurred (that the loved one is truly gone, etc.) p.53*

"It is not completely clear why this delay occurs. However, it most likely has to do with slower [Remember that retarded comes from the Latin word *tardus* which means "slow"] cognitive processing...It may simply take people with DS longer to recognize and understand...Anticipating this response can help prevent problems and prepare family and care providers to help with the grieving."*

We couldn't find out why he was bed-wetting and we couldn't understand why he was spitting at the mirror in the bathroom. What caused us the most concern were the blank stares he would constantly give us. We would beg him to tell us what was wrong but all we got was nothing.

"In our experience, this [Adam's] response is fairly common in people with Down syndrome who have experienced intense stress or emotional issues. That is, even if they are able to communicate with others about day-to-day issues, they may not be able to conceptualize and communicate more sensitive problems and issues. As a result, they may communicate these issues nonverbally through a change in behavior." p. 101 *

Adam eventually couldn't perform at work and had to quit before he would have been fired. He experienced extreme anxiety and continued talking about the "pokings" in the middle of his chest. In the book *Mental Wellness*... "One issue that was striking... was that [Adam] could not tell even close family members and staff what was happening to him, even though his world was turned upside down." p. 101 *

I must confess that I was disappointed at myself that I hadn't realized how Adam didn't have the adequate vocabulary to address something as complicated and elusive as these deep-rooted feelings. I should have taken the hint that whenever he answered my questions about what was wrong, he would respond, "I don't know". I now feel bad for losing my patience with Adam's constant denial of his condition and getting so upset by his moodiness. My wife explained, but did not condone, that I was upset because I'm a person who needs to fix things right away and grow thoroughly frustrated when solutions take longer than expected.

So, in conclusion, "Communication skills are vital to participating in society. Unfortunately, however, the expressive language problems of some people with Down syndrome create hurdles in daily life. Sometimes these problems can lead to misinterpretation of behavior of mental health problems. Sensitivity and patience on the part of family members and care providers improves mental health and improves the treatment of behavioral challenges" * p.103

To this day Adam is still not able to verbalize his eating OCD (Obsessive Compulsive Disorder) anxieties and, just recently, about not speaking loudly enough. I believe these are residual effects of all the stressors he went through and why he still needs a little bit of assurance from a clinical psychologist.

The need for ability to communicate is vital to one's existence. This should make common sense to everyone. Yet, it is not as evident to some people. For example, the school where I was teaching had special classes and classrooms for the deaf and hard of hearing. These students would exhibit at times aggressive behavior due to the frustration of not being understood by the hearing world. The inability to discern the words they couldn't hear would result in shrill cries of exasperation. Fortunately, the teachers in these special education classes understood that and were able to placate the students. Because of their behavior, some of the hearing students would poke fun at them and use the derogatory label "Binner!" whenever they wanted to insult their hearing classmates. Have you ever been so mad that you couldn't express yourself? Well, that's just the frustration many of those deaf students experience.

I can understand that even more so today. In our old age both my wife's and my hearing have deteriorated somewhat and hearing each other has become more difficult. As long as I can remember I have always been deaf in one ear. There are many times I will hear my wife, but ask her to repeat herself just because I want to make sure I heard correctly. We both become irritable when we have to repeat ourselves more often than ever now.

Thankfully, Adam is not overly frustrated by his inability to communicate his fears and accompanying anxiety, but he will become agitated if we push too hard on his eating issues. To this day I know that Adam still has fears that the "pokings" will come back. He has to be reassured that everything he is about to eat will "go together". Our young adult just doesn't have the critical thinking skills or the vocabulary to tell us what is wrong and why he is so concerned about eating. He does not deny that there is a problem, he just doesn't have the ability to tell us why. Yet, how many of us are in denial and unwilling to address some of the issues which visit our mental health, even when we have the vocabulary to express them. My psychologist friend at school told me once, "I will never be out of a job".

As of late Adam continues to go to a clinical psychologist every couple of months for help to overcome some residual OCD when it comes to eating. He does not have an eating disorder at present because he doesn't eat between meals, enjoys eating all kinds of food, and doesn't do junk food any more, while maintaining a healthy weight. Upon reflection, Barb and I think that Adam was overeating to comfort himself (like so many people do) over the misfortunes which visited his carefree world in those previous four months in 2010.

The fact that he was doing so much burping (we could hear it every night from this bedroom) should have been a clue that he was having indigestion. We thought it was Adam just losing his manners from the other end. Looking back, I should also not have been so busy working on research for the first book I was writing. What we flippantly called "bullfrogs on a lily pad" whenever we heard him belching in his room should have been loud and clear hints that something was wrong. The crumbs he left in the refrigerator were also clues that he was eating between meals, especially in the evenings.

VIGNETTE 17

THE APPLE OF OUR EYE ♣

The German word for eyeball is *Augapfel* which translates into "eye apple" In English anyone who is the "apple of my eye" is someone you are extremely proud and fond of. Adam fits that metaphor.

*32. Our 4-Leaf Clover with one of his
outside toys on a beautiful fall day*

Every parent thinks their child is special and, maybe that's the way things should be as long as that admiration is not unrealistically biased. Barb and I have had a life's worth of experience with children. As I noted before, Barb did child care for at least two decades. I shared 32 years of my life with junior high and senior high age students. We raised two other children who had to be guided through those trying prepubescent years... trying for all of us. When Adam came along we were seasoned citizens ready to take on a child who would need special help. As I've pointed out and exemplified before, with the exception of his physical problems, Adam had no problems with his socialization. He really was an exceptionally well-adjusted child and a pleasure to have around. That's why we were able to take him with us everywhere.

A case in point is the ability to laugh at himself without taking any offense. The Kelleesir was never overly sensitive and didn't mind being teased by Grandpa. Just as a reminder, it turned out to be a symbiotic relationship because, ironically, my Dad was able to learn to love unconditionally from someone who was labelled "learning disabled".

When my sister Erika was still alive, she echoed what I had known all along. When I was working on my first book *Passage:The Making of an American Family,* I had the opportunity to record her and ask her questions about her relationship with our father. At one point, she mused that Dad did not show the same kind of affection for her as he had for Adam. Here it is in her own words:

"However Dad mellowed a lot as he got older, and I believe the grandchildren played an important role in that transformation. I think Adam had a lot to do with that. Adam loved Grandpa and Dad could not be aloof and withdrawn with a special child who was persistently kissing him and throwing his arms around him. There was no way Adam was going to be denied, and there was no way Dad would deny him. Adam always thought Grandpa was the greatest".

I recently had a conversation with my brother Irv to tell him about *Four Leaf Clover*. I wanted to make sure that Barb and I were not overly biased about Adam's goodness. Because of their past history, it made only sense that I ask Irv his opinion of Adam. Without hesitation he quipped, "There's not a mean bone in his body. Adam and 'mean' just don't go together".

I can vouch for that because Adam even gets upset whenever I yell at our dog Babie. He thinks that it is mean to yell at her. Just like our father, my brother Irv also likes to tease Adam and make him laugh at his self-deprecating humor. On vacations and in warmer climes, my brother frequently gets out of his lawn chair and explains, "Stick a fork in me. I'm done already!". One of Adam's favorite Uncle Irv's quotes is, "I'm just one french fry short of a happy meal".

When it came to my sister Kathy's evaluation of Adam's character, she used the word "kind". She pointed out that he always asks how she and her husband Rollie are doing, and always complemented with a smile. She noted that he also has a dry sense of humor and likes to laugh. Finally, she has noticed that he likes to dance. I'm certain that An Exceptional Chorus has something to do with that.

Adam's older brother Jeff describes Adam as a "gentle soul". Jeff maintains that he always makes people feel good. And those feelings are undeniably honest because Adam wears them on his sleeve. Jeff acquired that insightful sentiment through experience living with our special person. If anyone should know Adam, it would be a brother who shared decades of experiences with him.

As far as his sister is concerned, we are keenly aware of Angela's love for Adam. Because of her and her husband Dwight, Adam will have a permanent home after Barb and I go to our final address. She has already been active with his care as well as ours. She is the main provider of respite care for us after Adam had his continuous psychological bout with acid reflux. She is also a teacher and, therefore, very attuned to people's needs. We are eternally thankful that Adam will be in good hands and in a loving home.

So, if Adam is not mean and, hence, a gentle soul, what then would be the one word to describe our son? That's easy: Love. But unlike the English language, which has only one word for love, the ancient Greeks had a wider concept of love and came up with additional words to better distinguish this all-important word which makes the world go round. They had 4 words for love:

- *Eros* which stands for romantic love
- *Philos* love for friends and humanity [Philadelphia - brotherly love]
- *Storge* love for family have come to the rea
- *Agape* unconditional "God" love

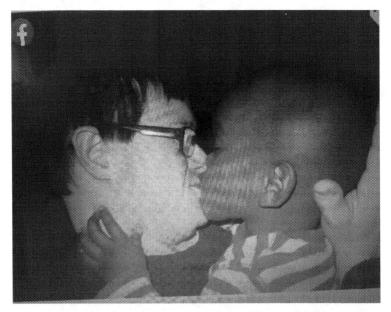

33. Adam showing some love to his nephew Carlos when he was just a youngster

It's not an exaggeration to say that Adam embraces and practices all of these four aspects of love. It is no coincidence then that Adam's favorite Holy Day is Christmas. Not because of the gifts he gets from family, but from the greatest gift all of us have received from God: love in the form of Jesus' birthday. God's love is unconditional and so is Adam's. To our benefit and others', Christmas also provides us with the opportunity to practice all four of these.

"Christmas is a necessity. There has to be at least one day of the year to remind us that we're here for something else besides ourselves" * Erik Sevareid reminded us years ago. It's just unfortunate that we don't practice this sentiment, if not the entire year, at least on more than just that one day in December.

Another way we can all show kindness to is to be civil to each other. We were so pleased to hear Adam say "yes, please" and "thank you". two phrases he used as soon as he started talking. His politeness is exemplary and frequently brings a smile to the recipients of that thoughtfulness.

Whenever Barb or I would go shopping he never begged or bugged for anything in the store. At times we would even have to ask him if he wanted anything special. The majority of times he would say, "No, Thanks". His selflessness always made us look at ourselves and what we value.

When asked to do something, he consistently follows through. Since I can no longer do things I used to be able to, Adam has become "Johnny on the spot", and does all the heavy lifting for me. He also is great at finding our glasses, our snacks, and our TV remotes during our couch potato sessions,

When we moved in the summer of 2020, Adam was a God-send. We had accumulated 32 years of 'things" at our home on the south side of Milwaukee. He helped pack most of them. Then he carried and moved boxes into the garage. He took all the things we weren't taking along and put them on our front lawn for anyone to pick up. Because of the Covid virus, Goodwill, and St. Vincent de

Paul were not accepting anything. All of the 100 or more boxes of books, pictures, albums, and other memorabilia were unpacked at our new home by him. He is still helping me now, at the writing of this book, with the Christmas decorations.

He has a moral compass, a term that has become almost a cliche today. However, in Adam's case, this cliche is apropos. He does not curse or use profanity. He follows the precept that cursing is the crutch of a conversational cripple. He prides himself in his personal wholesomeness, which shows that the quality of our thoughts is reflected by the quality of our language.

Whenever he feels he has been rude or inconsiderate, he might not apologize right away, but will always come back later to do just that. Again, just a delayed symptom of being a Downs person. His contrition will always be genuine and sometimes accompanied with tears of regret. He is the epitome of humility

Nobody's perfect, and as Adam is getting older, he sometimes gets grouchy. Since Barb and I are not perfect either, we are reminded that age will take a mental as well as a physical toll on us. The mental scars he still wears only proves that Adam is just as "normal" as we are...*Que sera sera*

When I recently talked to his cousin Marty and asked him what his considered judgement of Adam was, with fondness in his voice, he replied, "He is a very bright, warm soul. All my memories of him are good ones. I remember how I loved wrestling with him."

I asked Adam's cousin, Evan, if there was one word which would describe his uncle, Evan responded that Adam exudes "warmth". He likes that Adam always has a smile for everyone. Incidentally, that smile is captured by the artistic portraiture of Adam done by his uncle, which graces the front cover of this book.

Well, there we have it. All of those testimonials and tributes prove that Adam is just about as "normal" (and that's a debatable concept) as anyone else--and above normal when it comes to character and decency. He has taught uso much, especially that character secures our destiny. We are so proud of our young man.❧ ❧

34. Adam with his very own extraordinary (ET) heartlight

♪ "Turn on your heartlight
Let it shine wherever you go
Let it make a happy glow
For all the world to see" ♪ * ~ Neil Diamond

EPILOGUE

LESSONS LEARNED ♣

"The two most important days in your life are the day you are born and the day you find out why". * ~Mark Twain

Viktor E. Frankl, a Holocaust survivor and author of the celebrated book *Man's Search for Meaning,* addresses the meaning of life, which I, like many others, searched for in my younger years. According to Frankl, that meaning "lies in finding a purpose and taking responsibility for ourselves and other human beings. By having a clear 'why' we can face all the 'how' questions of life... to make the world a better place." * This is a philosophy that was indispensably helpful with the "how" part after I discovered the "why" part. The epiphany I was blessed with was the realization I came to was that there was a real harmony produced by their inseparability.

At this point in my life, I have also come to the realization that I now have more yesterdays than tomorrows; therefore, my tomorrows need to be even more substantive. Fortunately, as I continue my life's journey, I have learned that my best days are not done because the wisdom I have gained in the passing years has continued to enrich my life and, therefore is something I can pass on as my legacy.

Moreover, I've noticed that time is relative; time keeps moving inexorably forward, while the past keeps slowly creeping backward. The past defines us, but need not control us. Adversity shapes our lives, but need not destroy us. There are lessons we've learned from our predecessors. We need to follow them if they are going to have any value. I am reminded by the famous boxer Muhanned Ali that, "A man [or woman] who views the world the same at the age of 50 as he did at 20 has wasted 30 years of his life".*

I have also come to the understanding that whatever successes I have had are a shared legacy. Those sacrifices my grandparents and parents made allowed my siblings and me to get a college education. Their many years of efforts and things they gave up enriched our lives and allowed our successes to come to fruition. Any work ethic I have is a reflection of what my parents showed me in their daily efforts and struggles. I learned from them that parenting is a work in progress. They taught me how to be a good person, someone with empathy. These lessons and values were continuously endorsed by my relatives, teachers, and good friends As I have already said: "nobody does it alone".

Finally, there is another way of looking at this advice. If you don't believe that our main purpose in life is to help our fellow humans, then at least follow the Dalai Lama's recommendation and do nothing to harm them. It was Sister Theresa who felt that God did not create the poor. She blames our greed for that human condition.

It is in this spirit that Adam lives his life and teaches us to do likewise. Most importantly, he has taught us that the 10 Commandments are not multiple choice, and even though he might not know them by heart, he still follows them, especially "Love thy neighbor as thyself". This is probably one of the hardest to obey and why it is considered a golden rule.

Upon doing research on this particular commandment I have found that my hunch was correct and Adam's attitude towards all people fall in line with the following:

"When asked which is the greatest commandment, Jesus replied, 'Thou shalt love the Lord thy God with all thy heart, and with all thy soul, and with all thy mind. This is the first and greatest commandment. And the second is like unto it. Thou shalt love thy neighbor as thyself. On these two commandments hang all the law and the prophets'." (Mt. 22: 37-40).*

"These, however, are not really two, but one single command, the spheres of operation of which are completely inseparable. He did say the second was like the first...There is no need for any other law--if you're sufficiently well-versed in logic and theology".*

This concept of neighborly love and love in general is voiced by Mother Theresa who said that if we wanted to promote world peace, we should go home and love our family. Because the Bible tells us so, we need to extend that familial love to others. I quickly learned that my students needed more praise and less criticism from me. Their actions and reactions reminded me of their tacit expectations: "We don't care how much you know, we want to know how much you care."

I believe that as adults we choose our words carefully because it's easier to build up a child than to repair an adult. Shamefully, too many parents and those in charge of children in our society are not doing this. The proof? We spend six times more on our prison system than on our educational system. We talk about a waste of money, and yet continue to incarcerate the poor more often than not.

Then there is the question of what difference there is between "I like you" and "I love you?" This is beautifully summed up by Buddha: "When you like a flower, you pluck it...when you love a flower, you water it daily. One who understands this, understands life".* That's why our marriage of 56 years is still a work in progress. As parents Barb and I are continually nurturing our relationship with all our children. In spite of it being in the last section of this book, it's foremost importance lies in the lessons learned. This epilog not only reflects the teacher in me, but also gives the reader the opportunity to turn some of the perceived negatives of Down syndrome into an existential positive. Hopefully, some of these will overlap to parents of handicapped children. The self-deprecating humor in this memoir serves only as comic relief for a serious subject.

To share my good fortune, I have turned to the world of social media where I share a blog called "Tuesdays with Adam" which appears almost weekly on Facebook. I have taken the idea from the notable 2002 novel (and later, a movie), *Tuesdays with Morrie,* The book is all about an old man, Morrie, a young man named Mitch, and life's greatest lessons. In a nutshell:

"Maybe it was a grandparent, or a teacher of a colleague. Someone older, patient and wise, who understood you when you were young and searching, and gave you sound advice to help you make your way through it. For Mitch Albom, that person was Morrie Schwartz, his college professor from nearly twenty years ago". *

The advice Morrie gives to his former student goes back to the theme that runs throughout this entire narrative on Adam. Morrie tells the young man, "The most important thing in life is to learn how to give out love and to let it come in". * Adam had taught that to my father and others who might have been hesitant to let the love in for fear of being hurt or turned away. It reminds me of a quote by the poet Tenyson: "It is better to have loved and lost than not to have loved at all".* Indeed, without love, what would give our lives any real meaning?

Again, as soon as some people see or hear the word "love" they find out the word has very limited meaning because there are different kinds of love. This is where Morrie hits home with me as he addresses this ambiguity about love to his young devotee by explaining that "there is no experience like having children...You cannot do it with a friend. You cannot do it with a lover. If you want the experience of having complete responsibility for another human being and to learn how to love and bond in the deepest way, then you should have children" *

I had numerous opportunities to give some advice about life to the students in my literature classes. I reminded them that good literature, even fiction, is news that is still news today. Good fiction is also true to life. They all should learn what works and what doesn't from the conflicts which the main characters encounter. The follow-up discussions allow me to introduce them to the three stages in life that everyone goes through.

The first is **dependence**: when we are children and have to rely on parents and adults to help us with our lives.

The second stage: when we want our total **independence** and think mostly only of ourselves.

The third and last stage: when we have achieved **interdependence**, where others are now able to depend upon us, like children, siblings, and older parents. This, of course, demands sacrifices. It is at this stage that we have achieved and earned the right to be called adults

I then explained to my students that if they wanted to be real heroes, they should raise decent children so that we can leave the world in a better place. Superheroes are fictitious and exist only in our minds, celebrities like athletes, movie and rock stars are not heroes either, even if they are wrongfully called that. Those who help others out of love without expectation of remuneration are our only true heroes. I don't know how many essays by my students I have read addressing the prompt, "Who is your hero?" The majority of the heroes they chose to write about were "my mom", "my dad", "my uncle", et al. And most of these themes would produce the same refrain: "Because [s/he] was always there for me"

To this day, I feel I did my best teaching whenever I got off the lesson plans and injected those topics which would relate to my students' lives. What good is information if nothing can be done with it, especially in today's multi-media world with an overabundance of useless information thrown at them? In these times, I feel my approach was more important than ever. Everyone wants their Wi-Fi at warp speed and students click through so much data that it has become more useless rather than useful.. while we are all starving for wisdom.

Besides being there for them there are many variables pertaining to child rearing that we can't merely pick up a book (just ask Dr. Spock) and think of it as a manual for parenting or by watching Dr. Phil. I learned this caveat early on after watching a film in an Ed Psych class at the university in 1965. It showed, in black and white, three-year-olds on a typical playground and how they interacted with each other. When the film was over, the professor asked what we should have learned from what we observed. One brilliant and somewhat sarcastic student put it all in a nutshell: "different children are different". The professor, who looked like an envelope with no address on it, was left entirely speechless.

"Here Morrie speaks of the specific type of love that comes with child rearing. He asserts that parenting produces a different type of love than one can have with any other person. By being completely responsible for another person's life, one loves in the deepest way because, as Morrie asserts elsewhere, love is giving to others, not what you get from others. In that sense, being a parent stands as the truest kind of love because parenting requires sacrifice and, at least, no obvious reciprocation".*

Material things have an expiration date and in many cases do not fill that void we are falsely told by marketers will satisfy our and our children's needs. Only love can fill that need. We live in a materialistic society. Everything is consumed quickly and then thrown away. I recall hearing a woman answer someone as to how she explained being married to the same person for 65 years. She responded that she lived during an era that, when things were broken, they were fixed and not discarded. I am saddened whenever I hear people talk about "starter marriages".

Morrie continues with this explanation on love: "As long as we can love each other, and remember the feeling of love we had, we can die without ever really going away. All the love you created is still there. All the memories are still there. You live on--in the hearts of everyone you have touched and nurtured." *

So, at the end of this memoir, maybe we have learned more about the importance of all kinds of love, especially the kinds Adam illuminates. We need to revisit how we have nurtured others, like our children, parents, siblings and grandparents. It is then how our children and others will remember us, and emulate us in order to become decent and compassionate citizens. If we want to leave a lasting legacy, we should practice being life-long parents. Only then can we feel more confident that we will not be forgotten. I hope that this book has shed some light on how we can do better at raising and understanding "different" children. We can't imagine life without Adam.

ADDENDUM

Coincidence or Convenience ??

I concluded writing this book on the afternoon of Jan. 21, 2021. Without knowing this, our daughter-in-law, Molly, posted this on Facebook that evening:

> Today is the 21st Day
> Of the 21st Year
> Of the 21st Century!
> Three 21s!

Which is notable in the Down Syndrome community as people with Down syndrome have 3 copies [Trisomy 21] of their 21st chromosome. How cool is that? So thankful for that 21st chromosome magic!"

SOURCE NOTES

PROLOGUE
1. "song lyrics four-leaf" google.com/search
5. "Robinson. Journal of Contemporary Anthropology p.20, Vol. II (2011) Docs. lib.purdue.edu
5. Dunn, Lloyd M. Editor. *Exceptional Children in the Schools: Special Education in Transition: Second Edition.* N.Y., Chicago, San Francisco: Holt Rinehart and Winston Inc., 1973
6. Merriam Webster 11th Collegiate Dictionary...on line
7. "Stand a Little Rain" lyrics-Nitty Gritty Dirt Band: Google Search

STAGE 1
11. "Brennan Manning: quote fancy.com>Brennan-Manning

STAGE 2
17. "Victor Hugo". www.goodreads.com>quotes> 99537
20-21. "Lauren Suval". Psychcentral.com UNC Jul.8 2018
21. "Lauren Suval". Surprising Psychological Value of Human Touch Psychcentral. Com UNC Jul.8 2018

STAGE 3
22. "Buddha quote". Hope is stronger than fear. wwwgoodreads. com>quotes

23. "President Joe Biden". Doctors...nurses. MSNBC Newsbreak. Oct.19 2020
25. "Familial Retardation". www.alleydog.com<glossary>definition>term
25. "Atlanta Study". Psychology. jrank.org
26. "Milwaukee, Wisconsin...control group". Psychology.jrank.org
28. "Eddie Cantor" It took me 20 years.....www.quotes.net>quote
28. "Dalai Lama". Prime purpose of life...www.brainyquote.com>Authors

STAGE 4
30. "Abraham Maslow". Awareness...www.goodreads.com>author>457087
32-33. Dunn, Lloyd M. Editor. *Exceptional Education in Transition:Second Edition* N.Y.. Chicago, San Francisco. Holt Rinehart and Winston Inc., 1973
33. "Deborah Fidler". The emergence of syndrome-specific personality profile in young children with Down syndrome-Abstract. Pubmed.ncbi.nih.gov.
33-34. "Carr 1985. Gibson 1978". Downs personality. https://library.down-syndrome.org/en.us/research practice.

STAGE 5
35. "Lao Tzu"> Depressed, anxious, at peace.www.redbubble.com>poster>Lao Tzu
35. "James Conan Bryant". Behold the turtle...google.com/search
41. "Ralph Nader". Humor. Google .com/search. In humor there is truth.

LIFE WITH ADAM

VIGNETTE 4: JOURNEY
52. "Mark Twain". Travel. www.openculture.com>2017/12
42. "St. Augustine" Travel. www.brainyquote.com>St. Augustine Quotes

VIGNETTE 5: HOLY EMANATIONS

59. "StevenWright". Going to church...www.pinterest.com> Quotes by season

VIGNETTE 6: TV OR NOT TV

63.. "Life Goes On". google.com/search?q Life Goes On

VIGNETTE 8: OOPS!

73. "Dr. Oz Show". .www.doctoroz.com>videos>embarrassing body functions

VIGNETTE 9: EXCEPTIONAL GROUP

76. "Friedrich Nietsche" Without music. google.com/search?q. Music quote
78. "An Exceptional Chorus 2009 Benefit Concert" booklet. America the Beautiful
81. "News at 10". WITI TV6 10 pm Newscast on Dec. 18, 2019

VIGNETTE 12: ALL IN THE FAMILY

91. "Michael J. Fox". Family. google.com/search. Michael Fox family quote
93-94. Schissler, John Jr. *Immigrants: A Passage Revisited.* Pp 63-64 Indiana, Xlibris,2017

VIGNETTE 13: OLDIES BUT GOODIES

100. "Steven Wright"107 Best of Steven Wright. Laughteronline university.com
99. "Ralph Nader" humor. google.com/search. In humor there is truth

VIGNETTE 14: RED LETTER DAYS

102. "Charlie Brown" Christmas Tree. google.com/search. Charlie Brown on Xmas

VIGNETTE 15: AVANT SAVANT

101 "Mark Twain" When I was 14...google.com/search...www. reddit.com

102 "Pam Allyn" Reading and Writing...google.com/search?q=reading+is

VIGNETTE 16: DEALING WITH LOSS

117-118. McGuire, Dennis PhD, and Chicoine, Brian, M.D. *Adults With Down Syndrome.* Woodbine House. Bethesda, MD. 2006

VIGNETTE 17: THE APPLE OF OUR EYE

124. "Erik Sevareid" Christmas. www.goodreads.com>quotes>11896

126. "Neil Diamond" Heartlight. google.com/search?q=neal+dia mond+heartlight+lyrics

EPILOGUE

127. "Mark Twain" Two Most Important Days. google.com/ search?q=mark+twain

127. Frankl, Viktor E. *Man's Search For Meaning.* Boston, Mass. Beacon Press, 1992

127. "Mohammed Ali". 30 years of life...www.goodreads. com>quotes>41409

128. *Bible.* google.com/ search. Greatest Commandment. Love Thy Neighbor.Matthew 22:36-40

129. *Bible.* Greatest commandment. www.biblegateway.com>passage

129. "Buddha Quote" flower. google.com/search. www.pinterest. com...wordshurt

130. "Morrie Quotes" www.goodreads. Study Notes for *Tuesdays With Morrie*

130. "Alfred Lord Tennyson" Tis better to have loved. google.com/ search?q=better+ to+have+loved.

130. "Morrie Quotes" www.goodreads. Sparknotes. On children*Tuesdays With Morrie*

1132-133."Morrie Quotes" www.goodreads. Sparknotes. On forgotten *Tuesdays With Morrie*

Printed in the United States
By Bookmasters